How to Look After Yourself First

10 Steps to Looking After You First

Shane Lopez

contained within this document, including, but not limited to, errors, omissions, or inaccuracies.

Table of Contents

Introduction

Self-care has recently become a big topic in the mainstream media. We hear people talking about it all the time. Unfortunately, the way it is presented may lead many people to believe that self-care is actually a selfish act, but this is a myth. Self-care is not selfish; in fact, it is one of the best things you can do for yourself and others. The problem is that most people don't know what it is or how to implement it in their own lives.

Are you the type of person who is always getting asked to do other people favors? Things like letting them borrow your money, doing their tasks for them, or going the extra mile for others. These are all great things, but they can lead to you being burnt out. The truth is that you cannot give your all to every person that asks something of you. This will leave you very drained, and you will have no time for yourself. Nobody will take care of you if you don't prioritize it for yourself. You have to be the one to take care of yourself, and it can't be a secondary thought. It has to be something that you do before you even think about helping others.

I know this might be a foreign concept for many, but it is important to consider and understand. Self-care is all about making yourself a better person to interact with those around you more effectively. This book is designed to take you through self-care and how to implement it. It will teach you why it is essential and how you can improve in your capacity. You won't even have to spend more than 30 minutes a day going through this book to improve your life. It should take you about a month to get through it, and you will feel empowered to make a change. A small commitment to spending some time on yourself and reading through this book can be the thing that completely changes your life.

If you are constantly helping people first, it can be a huge problem. It hinders your growth, and it makes you the least important person in your own life. I want you to become the main character in your own story and take back control of your life. If you think that it is not possible, I am here to tell you that it is. I know this because I have personal experience with it, as I have coached and mentored people who would lend money to family and be stuck in a position of not being able to pay the bills they needed to. People who would work so hard to please other people that they let their personal life slip. I have seen what it can do to people, but I also know how to fix it.

Over the years, I have been a teacher and mentor who has helped people to learn to love and support each other in a healthy way. You do not want to be in a position where you give everything to the other person and have nothing for yourself. I help support people in the journey to learning to love themselves so that they are able to love others. It is important that every person knows how to live healthy lives and have healthy relationships.

Once you have gone through this book, you would have the skills to live a life that you are happy with. You will be able to tell people no respectfully and assertively. You will no longer be taken advantage of. You will exude confidence and have the self-esteem needed to know what you are worth to the world. People who know their worth will not be taken advantage of. They will only do the things that they deem worth their time, and they can love people in the right way.

I have worked with many people, so I know how to find solutions to many problems that deal with self-care. The people who have accepted and learned from my mentorship now have a much more solid and robust mindset that pushes them forward in life. They can find out what they want from life and chase after those goals with all they have. I have seen people go from timid to so self-confident that you can feel their presence when they walk into a room, and you can also have this transformation. Picking up this book is the first step. After that, you just need to implement the things that you have learnt along the way. Of course, there will be work that needs to be done from your side, but

I am confident that you will look after your finances, health, inner self, body, and mind with my guidance.

There is a saying that goes, "Looking out for yourself is not selfish. Looking out for yourself is knowing that you can't help anyone if you can't help yourself." This is what we are going to be basing everything in this book on. It is about knowing how to look after yourself first. Once you get that right, you will be able to work on looking after others.

As you read through this book, you will be given actionable steps to use in your life. There are real-world examples that will help you understand how you should implement certain things and show you how specific actions hurt you and others. By the time you close this book, I want you to be better than what you are now. This is possible if you are willing to learn and grow throughout this journey. Each chapter takes a step forward, focusing on something specific that you can do and change in your life to make yourself a better person and improve the quality of your life. You need to learn how to take care of yourself first!

Chapter 1:

Focusing on Yourself – Basics You

Need to Know About!

It can be very easy to get caught up trying to meet everyone else's needs. You can get so swept up in a whirlwind of taking care of others that your own needs take a back seat. Taking care of others is important, but it can only be done when you are fully taken care of, which many of us miss. We get so focused on making sure everyone else is doing okay that we just never check in with ourselves.

We all need relationships with others. As humans, we all crave companionship and real relationship and intimacy. This is a completely normal need, but you should never make it so important that you do not focus on the other aspects of yourself. Most people think that their relationships will suffer if they focus on themselves, but this is not necessarily true, and you can have both. The truth is that if you focus on yourself first, your other relationships will benefit from it as well.

Why is it so Important to Focus on Yourself?

Your relationship with yourself is the most important relationship you will ever have. The way you treat yourself reflects what you think of yourself, and all other relationships will build off the relationship you have with yourself. We all have insecurities, but if we do not deal with them, it can affect how we see ourselves and interact with others.

We tend not to like people who have the characteristics we dislike in ourselves. I'm sure that there is someone you have complained about in your life, only for someone to tell you how similar you two are. This happens because we do not like to see our weaknesses in other people, so very similar people tend to irritate us the most. This might create strife in relationships, which is why loving yourself and taking care of yourself should always be your first priority.

Why You Matter First

When you recognize that you need to take care of yourself first, you acknowledge that you are important. You are choosing to pay attention to your needs and will do your best to meet them. All too often, we get stuck in a cycle of not paying attention to our needs. We focus so much on the external that the internal gets neglected.

We matter first because we can never be effective at being there for others unless we have taken care of ourselves. Have you ever been on an airplane? If so, you have probably heard the safety speech. The cabin crew usually gives a rundown of what to do in an emergency to ensure that you are prepared. Each person has an oxygen mask that will be dropped down should something happen to the plane while it is in the air. The rule is to put your mask on first before you help someone else with theirs; even if the person next to you is unconscious or unable to put their oxygen mask on for some reason, you never help them before you have put your mask on first. This might sound selfish to many people, but it is the only way to make sure that both you and the other person are safe. Lack of oxygen can lead to you not being able to think straight, and you will start to feel much weaker, so if you try and put the other person's mask on first, you will risk not being able to help them and yourself. If you put your mask on first and ensure that you are getting oxygen, you will have the clarity of mind, energy, and physical ability to help the other person.

This is the same principle that should be followed in every person's life. It might seem heroic and selfless to help the other person first, but you actually end up harming both of you in the process. You will never be able to give your all to another person if you have not taken care of yourself first. This is an important life lesson and needs to become a norm in every person's life. You should never feel guilty for taking care of yourself because this will allow you to be the best person you can be for other people.

The people around you are essential. They should be so important to you that you make sure that you know that you matter first. You cannot pour out of an empty cup. If you want to be effective in any area of life, you must fill yourself up first, and then you can focus on filling other people up and taking care of them.

You matter just as much as any other person. You have value in your life, and you should be treating yourself as such. Something that I have realized is that people will only treat you as well as you treat yourself. If you treat yourself like you don't matter, you give other people the right to do the same. You will find that people who are confident and know their worth almost immediately gain the respect of other people, while people who constantly put themselves last are treated the same way by those around them. We all want to be treated well, and the secret to this is to treat yourself well.

The Best Approach to Learning How to Focus on Yourself

If you have always put others ahead of yourself, focusing on yourself might not come naturally, but it is a skill that anybody can learn. To focus on yourself, you must find out what you need, and you must get to know yourself better since you will never be able to take care of yourself properly if you are not adequately acquainted with yourself. This might sound like a strange concept. Most people believe that they know themselves pretty well, but in actuality, they know themselves the least out of all the people they have relationships with. This is because if you don't put intentional effort into getting to know yourself, you will never truly be able to.

I'm sure there are people in your life who you see all the time without really knowing them. You might pass them at work and say hi, but that is the extent of your relationship. On the other hand, other people live miles away from you, but you have made an effort to connect with them, and those people could be the closest to you. This proves that proximity does not mean that you know someone or have a good relationship with them. The same is true of your relationship with yourself. Just because you are always around yourself does not mean that you know yourself.

In order to truly get to know yourself, you have to put in the effort. It will take some work from your side, but the end goal will be worth it. There are plenty of things that can be done in an effort to get to know yourself. These things are essential because they will open up new self-discovery doors and help you build up your relationship with yourself. You do not have to do all of them simultaneously; instead, pick one or two and focus on them. If you want to amp it up, you can take on another one. This process will make it more sustainable. Eventually, these things will become a habit that you just do because you enjoy it and become part of your everyday life.

Keep a Journal

Journaling is a great way to find out some new things about yourself since it is a chance to get everything in your head down on paper. Unfortunately, we often do not take the time to acknowledge our thoughts since our schedules can get busy, and our thoughts and feelings can get lost in all of that. However, it is important to take the time to acknowledge our thoughts and feelings to know ourselves better and help get out anything we are holding onto.

Keeping a journal that you write in every day is a great way to express yourself safely, and you will also be able to look back on what you have written in the past. A journal helps you to get a broad view of your thoughts and feelings. You will pinpoint specific events or time frames where you have been feeling a certain way. If you need to adjust something in your life, you can do that based on your knowledge from going back in your journal.

Writing in your journal is just as important as reading what you have written back to yourself. You need to do both of these things in order to get the full benefit of journaling. You should also be as consistent as possible with your journaling. It can be a relaxing experience, so it is a great thing to do before bed. This is usually the ideal time because you get to reflect on your day and get out any frustrations you may be feeling. You could also journal in the morning if you feel up to it. This time will help you set up your expectations for the day, and it is always a good idea to spend some quality time with yourself in the morning.

Check-In With Yourself

The business of the day often gets away with us, and we do not take the time to check in with ourselves. Checking in lets, you take some time to pause and ask yourself how you are feeling and see if there is anything that may have caused the negative or positive emotions. When there is a significant shift in the way you are feeling, it is beneficial to take some time to analyse this. You will get to know yourself better by pinpointing what is causing these emotional and mood shifts.

It doesn't take long to do this or require a lot of effort. First, you have to pause and ask yourself how you feel and what is causing those feelings. Then, if you want to take it a step further, you can write a quick note about it on a small notebook that you can carry with you or on your phone. Then, when you sit down to journal at the end of the day, you will also be able to look back on these events.

Make a List of Experiences You Want to Have In Your Life

The experiences we desire to have will tell us a lot about ourselves. For example, we can figure out how we want our loves to look, and this is valuable information about ourselves. Think about when you meet someone for the first time. There are lots of questions that you can ask to get to know them, but one of the most popular ones is, "What do you do for fun?" We ask this because we can almost immediately tell whether the person is adventurous, likes to take risks, prefers to stay at home and have a quiet lifestyle, or enjoys being productive with their hobbies. From this, we can gauge whether or not we will be able to get along with this person as a close friend.

You should be doing the same with yourself. Ask yourself what you like to do and see what similarities you can draw from that. This will also help you take part in things you enjoy, as you will focus on the experiences that add joy to your life. This will also allow you to meet people who want the same things as you, which will add to your life quality.

Try Something New Each Day

In some cases, we do not know what we like to do. Luckily, as long as we take the time to figure it out, this is okay. As we grow older, we change as people, meaning that you will not be the same person now as you were in your teens, and you will also be a different person in the next 10 years. This is the natural progression of life. The things you used to enjoy are just not as enjoyable as they were, and you now find different things that you like to do. The problem is that most people do not take the time to assess themselves and find out new things that fit into their stages of life, lifestyle, and personality. This is why you will find that as people get older, they stop having hobbies and doing fun things. It is not that they do not want to have this in their life, but they simply do not know what to do.

The trick is to try something new each day. This does not have to be anything big. Taking a different route to work, wearing something you would not usually wear, or speaking to someone you usually just pass by are all new. These things will help you to grow and become a better person. This also gets you used to trying new things that are bigger and more intimidating. You can then incorporate a bigger new thing weekly or monthly. New experiences always show us more about ourselves than we think.

Find Out Your Likes and Dislikes

What we like or dislike tells us a lot about ourselves and our values, and it also gives us a window into situations we should put ourselves in and ones that we should avoid. Most of the time, we know what we like and dislike, but there are times when things can fall through unnoticed. If you have any particularly positive or negative emotions in any scenario, you should stop and acknowledge them. Then, find out what made you have these emotions, which will help you find out the root of your likes and dislikes.

Write Down Your Strengths and Weaknesses

Acknowledging our strengths and weaknesses is a powerful way to get to know ourselves, as it helps us be realistic with where we are and what we are capable of. Every person has different strengths and weaknesses, and if you allow yourself to play to these, you will be able to make better choices and decisions. We have to know where our strengths lie because if we know that we will perform better in certain scenarios, we can focus on making ourselves better in these areas and will be able to choose things that we enjoy. Our strengths often lead us to what we enjoy, which will help us choose careers, hobbies, and anything in between.

It is also important to acknowledge your weaknesses. We rarely like to face our weaknesses as they can be perceived as the negative aspects of ourselves. This is true in some cases, but it can also lead us to find out the things we should just not give our time to. There are certain weaknesses that should be worked on to make ourselves better, but there are other weaknesses that we should just accept. For example, if you notice that you are impatient, unforgiving, or unfocused, these weaknesses can be worked on. These are things that will add to your life, and they can be improved upon with a little bit of work. Other weaknesses, such as not having a particular talent like singing or dancing or not being a good writer or public speaker, are things you might just not be naturally good at.

Instead of forcing yourself into career paths or choosing hobbies that highlight these weaknesses, you can choose something in your strengths. For example, if you are naturally great with numbers, you can choose to do more things that include this trait and leave the public speaking to someone more gifted in this area. In these cases, it is better to focus on building up your strengths to be even better rather than trying to build up your weaknesses. You will excel even more when you spend time on your strengths since the ceiling for your weaknesses is usually lower, and it will be challenging to be better than someone who has a natural power for that thing.

Knowing your strengths and weaknesses is very powerful because you will put yourself in situations that allow you to shine. You have to be honest with yourself and really think about what you are good at and what you lack in. If you struggle to pinpoint these things, you can ask someone you trust to give you, their opinion. They will be able to see things that you may have missed.

Finding Out What You Want From Life

To truly take care of yourself, you will need to know what you want out of life. Unfortunately, many people do not know what they want from their lives, making it difficult to be happy and truly live a life they enjoy. This is why it is important to do this before focusing on other areas of your life.

Learn to Be Selfish

The word selfish sounds… well, selfish. It is not a word that is used to compliment someone, so it sounds like something negative. While excessive selfishness is a bad thing and will probably cost you most of your relationships, you do need some level of selfishness in your life. Selfishness is when you think of yourself first, meaning you think about what is best for you, and then you do that thing. If you are completely unselfish, you will never choose what is suitable for you and will always be putting others above yourself.

You need some level of selfishness in order to find out what you want out of life. While taking care of others and putting their needs first is noble, it is often unsustainable, especially in the case of trying to figure out what you want out of life. You will never be able to figure out what you truly want out of life if you are constantly sacrificing your time and resources for others. Instead, take the time to sit down with yourself and ask, "If I had no other responsibilities, what would I want to do with my life?" This is a powerful question because it will lead you to find out where your passion lies. You may not be able to drop everything and chase that dream, but you will be able to see where your passions lie and find a way to get there. Being selfish is not about dropping all of your responsibilities. It is about looking within yourself and finding out what will make you happy.

Find Out What Really Bothers You

Sometimes, finding out what we want is not a clear-cut path. It can often take us to figure out what we do not like and what upsets us to pinpoint what we want out of life. In order to do this, you have to look at your life and where you are right now and find the things that get under your skin and upset you. These are going to be the things that you want to change. It could be anything, including a micromanaging boss, feeling meaningless at work, or being drained from day-to-day tasks. If you know what bothers you, you will see what you need to change.

Knowing what you do not like will give you something to push back against, which could propel you significantly. If you think of any person who has done something significant in their life, it was because they had a problem and they wanted to fix it. People create inventions and platforms to solve problems and do something they enjoy and have a vision for. If you are looking to get to know yourself better and find out what you want from life, finding out what bothers you might be the key.

Determine What Makes You Truly Happy

It is easy to feel like we are just wasting our life away. When we get stuck in the rut of just waking up, going to work, and coming back home just to get ready to do it all again, we can lose our happiness. Finding out what makes you happy will allow you to get to the root of your desires. Do you find happiness when you are around children? Do you love spending time around animals? Does planning and creating strategies make you feel useful and happy? Does being your own boss spark joy in you? Do you want to travel or be financially free? There are so many things that could make you happy, and you just have to do the legwork to figure it out.

Once you know what makes you happy, you will know what direction you want your life to be moving in. You will then have a clear idea of what you want out of life and what you should be striving for. In order to get to know yourself and to know what you want out of life; you need to know what makes you happy and what sparks joy in your life. Then, you will be able to plan to have more of that in your life so that you feel more fulfilled and more excited about every day.

Chapter 2:

How to Train Yourself to Say NO!

It can be so easy to say yes to things. In fact, it is almost expected that we say yes when we are asked to do something. Yes, is not the only option here, however, as it's always ok to say no to things. Saying yes to too many things can actually be harmful in the long run, as it will stop you from focusing on yourself and eventually burn you out.

Different Ways of Saying No

People do not like to say no because they feel as though it will be too harsh. We all want others to like us, and we do not want to upset others most of the time. While this is a nice sentiment, it is not healthy if we are saying yes, all the time. You have to have boundaries in your life that allow you to say no in the right way. If you do not know how to say no, then you have come to the right place. I will teach you lots of ways in which you can say no, be firm, and still be respectful.

The art of saying no is a skill that needs to be built in every person. You don't even have to explain why you are saying no. Most people do not need an explanation from you. Sure, you should not overdo it and go around telling everyone no, but you need to have boundaries, and things that fall into those boundaries need to be said no to. If you commit to having dinner with your family, and someone from work asks you to stay late and help them with a project, you have the right to say no. No should also be used when you have made a commitment to yourself. If someone asks you to do something, but you are exhausted and know that you need to take some time for yourself, you should be able to say no and not give an explanation. The problem with trying to have an answer for every time you say no is that the other person will not think your excuse is as vital as the thing, they need help with. It can be difficult to justify yourself, so it is often best to say no and not offer an explanation.

The other thing about saying no is that it does not mean no forever. Just because you can't do it now does not mean that you will never be able to do it. People often want you to do things immediately, but this will often not be something you can do, especially if you have other commitments to yourself and others. You can say no but offer to do it another time that suits you best, or you could also contribute to help if you have the capacity to do so partially. The trick is to know what you can do and then only offer that. You should always know your boundaries so that you can say no to keep people from overstepping, which keeps you from breaking your boundaries for the cause of others.

There are tons of ways you can say no, and they will fit every scenario. If you do not want to use the simple "no," then here is a list of ways in which you can say no:

- Not now.
- No thanks, I won't be able to make it.
- Unfortunately, I can't fit another thing into my schedule.
- I won't be able to right now, but I might be able to [insert day or time here].
- I can't help, but I do know someone who is more well-suited. Let me ask them and get back to you. (If you do this, please make sure that the other person will help and then ask them first before handing over their contact information.)
- You are so kind to think of me, but I won't be able to join you.
- That sounds great, but I have another commitment.
- I have a lot of work to do and will not be able to.
- Can we take a raincheck on that?
- I just need to take some time for myself, so I can't.
- I'm not taking on any new things at the moment.
- Perhaps we could do it another time?

- I'm not sure that I am the best fit for this.
- No, thank you, but it sounds lovely.
- I can't.
- I am not able to set aside the time needed.
- I'm so honored but won't be able to.
- I wish I could, but it is not going to work at this time in my life.
- Sadly, I have something else on.
- Thank you so much for asking. Can you keep me on the list for next time?
- I will have to pass this time around.
- No, sorry, that isn't really my thing.
- Can I get back to you with my answer?
- The demands would be too much for me at this time.
- No!

As you can see, there is an infinite number of ways to say no. It doesn't matter what their situation is, as you will always have the choice to say no. You can use the ones that are listed here or make up your own ones. The key is to be firm and to communicate the right thing. If it is only a no for the time being, then you should let the other person know that. If you never intend to say yes, then communicate that to the person. If you want to fulfil the person's request but cannot, you can let them know. Doing this will allow you to be polite but firm at the same time. It will also let the other person know where you stand.

Why You Should Learn to Say 'No' More Often

Saying no is an essential skill that must be learned if you want to live a life filled with the things you value and want to enjoy. People who do not say no are often taken advantage of because others know they will always be willing to do something for them. This is not a healthy way to live because we have our own lives with our own responsibilities. These things should always take priority over what other people expect of us. There are so many benefits and reasons you should be saying no. Let's go through some of them here.

You Have a Say in What Your Life Looks Like

You empower yourself to make choices better aligned with your dreams and goals when you can say no. You remove the confusion of where your priorities lie and can take charge of your life. When you allow yourself to be available to everyone who wants you there, you make their priorities eclipse yours. You are essentially choosing to better someone else's life and leave yours to remain mediocre. You are the one living your life, which means you have to make a life that you want to live.

You only have a limited amount of time, resources, and energy in the day, and you have to decide how to use it. If you use the majority of it on yourself, you will see your life move forward, and you will be able to build the life you want. However, if you use most of it on other people, they will take all the benefits because they do not have to do as much work. This is not what you want. This is why you need to have your priorities in place so that you can say no for the right reasons.

You Don't Have to Be Overly Stressed

Life can be overwhelming and stressful, even more so when you are constantly saying yes to everything. Even if you love your job, there needs to be boundaries in place so that you can have some time for yourself. Being able to say no is the best way to create balance in your life. No person can work all the time, as we all need some time to take a break and do something fun.

If you are someone who always says yes and is always available, you might find that you end up overcommitting yourself. Evaluate why you are saying yes and make sure that it is for the right reasons and not letting another part of your life suffer for your commitment. If you are known as the person who always says yes, it will take some time for you to build up your boundaries to a point where people do not take advantage of you. This is where you need to be quite firm with your noes so that people understand that there are limits to what you will agree to. When you can say no to the right things and give yourself time to relax, you will feel much less stressed.

You Gain Confidence and Respect

When you can say no, you recognize how valuable your time and resources are because you will only say yes to things worth giving that up. People notice this, and you gain respect for it. We can think that the best way to earn respect from people is to be available for them and agree to what they want from us, but the opposite is true. People who always say yes are usually undervalued because people will pass on things, they do not want to do to someone else. If you are that person for them, you allow them to put responsibilities on you that they think are below them.

Saying no also increases your confidence because you can stand up for yourself and put boundaries in place. Saying no does not mean that you do not want to put in the effort to help someone, but that you value your promises enough to want to put in the necessary action to make sure that it is done correctly and to the best of your ability. If you cannot give this time and attention to the task, then it is best to say no. This shows that you are confident in your abilities and know where your priorities lie. The confidence and respect you will earn from saying no to the right things go hand in hand.

You Start Making Time For the Things That Matter

One of the quickest ways to fail is to try and please every person in your life all the time. I can tell you for a fact that it is impossible to do so, and therefore should not even be attempted. When you say no to others, you open doors to say yes to opportunities that will take you forward. Learning to say no is part of growing and improving, meaning that you will achieve your goals in life much more effectively.

This also means that you need to learn to say no to yourself. You will not want to do some things in life because there seems to be something a little easier that is more attractive. In these moments, you have to say no to yourself and do the hard things. You need to have boundaries with yourself and be firm with what you want. Saying no will enable you to be more resilient and push through to the more important and beneficial things. Saying no might be hard to say to other people, but it can be even harder to say to yourself.

When you have developed the skill of saying no, you will intentionally say yes to the right things and the things that matter to you. This could be working on your business idea, spending time with your family, focusing on your health, studying, working on a hobby, or anything important to you. The less important things will take a backseat as you drive forward to make your life look the way you want it to look. Saying yes and no to the right things really does have the power to change your life.

Dealing With People Who Won't Take 'No' for an Answer

You will experience a few people who simply cannot take no for an answer. These people are usually trying to manipulate you into doing what they want you to do. They can be doing this on purpose or unconsciously, but you should not fall for it either way. They do not have your best interest at heart because they were not respecting your answer when you said no.

Most people who are being manipulative in some way do not know they are doing it. This is usually because they have not had healthy boundaries and behaviours modeled for them, and they are just following what they have experienced. This does not make them bad people, but it means that you will have to be a lot firmer with these people. It is not your place to change the way people do things unless they have invited you into that space into their lives. Most people do not respond to corrections very well, especially if you do not have a close relationship with them, so it can be best to focus on your response instead of their actions.

When someone is trying to get their way with you, they might start expressing feelings of fear, anger, or even panic. The reason for this is that they are trying to control the situation the best they can. This is a form of emotional manipulation, and you should not fall for it. Whenever someone asks you for something, and you can't do it, you should be honest and say no in any way we have discussed or in a way that works best for you. If you sense that the person is not taking no for an answer and has started trying to manipulate you, it is time to kick it up a notch.

Remember that the person is probably unaware that they are manipulating you, so there is no need to be rude or harsh with your response. However, you need to make it clear to them that they are manipulating you somehow and that you are still going to stand firm with your answer. If this person is someone whom you are close with, you do not want to ruin the relationship with something harsh. so, try to simply allude to the manipulation rather than accusing them of it. For example, you can say something along the lines of, "In the past, I have said yes when I did not want to. I would like to feel like I am being heard and my needs are being met. If you are willing to meet me halfway and compromise, then we can continue discussing this." This is firm and lets them know exactly where you stand, but it is also not rude. In most cases, the other person will take what you have said and apologize. You can then move forward from here, hopefully to where you can both have an outcome that works for you.

While this does work in most cases, you might be faced with someone who is just not listening to what you have to say. These people will continue with their agenda, and while this can be frustrating for you, don't give in. You also shouldn't be rude and blow up, as this could make the situation worse for the both of you, and it's always best to avoid a fight. You can respond to them by saying, "I don't feel like you are listening to what I have to say or taking my feelings and needs into consideration. If you are not willing to meet me halfway or discuss in a way that could work for both of us, then I am afraid we will have to stop this conversation right here and come back when you are ready to compromise and hear me out." This shows that you are not going to budge and that you will walk away should the conversation continue in the way it has been going. If you see that they are still not listening, tell them that you will remove yourself from the conversation because this isn't going to work for you, and then do just that. Do not stay in a situation where you are being manipulated, and the other person will not let up. This is the best way to handle manipulative people and to make sure that you still get an outcome that will work for you.

Remember that you do not have to yell or respond rudely to the other person, as this could just light a flame in them and make the conversation even worse. You should always aim to handle things calmly so that nothing can be pointed back to you.

Chapter 3:

What Is Self-Care?

Self-care is crucial, and I think it is something that most of us do not do as much as we should. Yet, we all need to take care of ourselves because you are the only person that truly has your best interest at heart all the time. When you prioritize self-care, you will find that your mood will improve significantly, and you will feel energized and ready to tackle whatever comes your way. We can all find some time in our schedules for self-care; in fact, it should be a necessity to do so.

What is Self-Care?

In today's culture, the words "self-care" is often associated with treating yourself to lavish items and days out. You see this all the time on social media, but this is extreme and not really what self-care is all about. Of course, it is nice to do this once in a while, but it does not lend itself to the type of self-care we will be talking about in this chapter.

Proper self-care is a daily ritual where you are making sure that your needs are met. If you think of when parents bring home their baby from the hospital, that baby is now in their care. They will have to do everything in their power to make sure that the baby's needs are met. This is because the baby cannot do this for themselves, and it needs to be taken care of in order for the baby to grow up happy and healthy. The parents have to do a lot of things for the baby, such as feed it, bathe it, change dirty diapers, put it to bed, make sure that the baby is conformable, entertain the baby, and make sure that it is feels loved, and many other things. Once the baby has grown up, all of those responsibilities fall on it because it would be old enough to take care of itself.

The problem is that we tend to not take care of ourselves in the same way we would care for others. What comes as second nature for us to do for babies and others, we hardly ever do for ourselves. This is why self-care is so important, as we have to meet our own needs to be happy and healthy. The World Health Organization states that the fundamental principles of self-care are self-reliance, empowerment, autonomy, personal responsibility, and self-efficacy (2018). It means being able to take care of yourself and provide for yourself in every aspect of your being, including physically, emotionally, and spiritually. Let's talk about all three of these aspects.

Physical

Physical self-care is taking care of your physical surroundings and your physical body as well. You have to make sure that both of them are good, clean, and healthy. Your physical health plays a significant role in your mental and emotional health; if you cannot take care of yourself physically, then there is a massive chance that you will not be able to take care of the other aspects of yourself.

A range of activities could include taking care of yourself physically, including cleaning up the space around you, doing laundry, organizing your things, brushing your teeth, taking care of your skin, eating healthy, and exercising. As you can see, this is a pretty broad list of things that can be done to improve your physical health. You should also see your doctor for annual checkups and do something that will make your body physically healthier and stronger.

Taking care of yourself is essential. It would help if you had basic physical care processes to keep sicknesses and diseases at bay. This will contribute to a long and healthy life, which is something that we all want. Usually, it can be easy to let your physical health dive into stress or sadness; since physical care is all about taking action, it is difficult when you do not feel like it. I would say that developing a routine and sticking to it is one of the best things you can do. A routine will be the thing you default to without even having to think about it. Place a few physical care steps in your routine, and you will be able to do it without much mental energy being used up.

Emotional

Emotional self-care is the cornerstone of all self-care. Our emotions impact the way we see the world and how we interact with it, and if we are not emotionally taken care of, it is tough to be as effective as we should be. So, I would stress that you should focus on taking care of yourself emotionally because you can only do this. Others can help take care of you physically in desperate circumstances, but your emotions are only something you have access to, which needs to be a priority.

To take care of yourself emotionally, you need to be in tune with your needs and do things you deem meaningful. Your emotional health can also be taken care of when you spend time unwinding and relaxing. We all need time to be with our thoughts, which helps us take care of our emotional well-being. Some activities that you could try are yoga, massage, taking a bath, journaling, meditation, and socializing with people you enjoy being around. You could also spend time doing a hobby that you find interesting. There is nothing better than sitting down and doing something that you like doing. There are no rules here; as long as you like it and find that you are getting joy from it, you will be adding to your emotional health.

What works for you will be completely different from what will work for someone else. It all comes down to personal taste and personality, which is why you usually can't take what someone else does to take care of their emotional health and copy/paste it into your life. It is much better just to allow yourself to figure it out. You may have to spend some time trying different things, but you will eventually land on a few activities that you can do to take care of yourself emotionally. Remember that it all starts with finding things that you enjoy and things that feel meaningful to you. You can even look to the things you used to do as a child for guidance since our childhood hobbies often lead us to what we really care about.

Spiritual

When I talk about the spiritual aspect of self-care, I refer to connecting with your inner being or to a higher power if you are religious. The point of spiritual self-care is for you to connect with that side of yourself, and there are lots of things that you can do for this, which will vary depending on your beliefs and the type of religion you subscribe to. When you do this, you are working on your personal development, peace, and the foundation for your beliefs and values. Many people do not take enough time to focus on this, but it is crucial since it has shaped you to be the person you are now.

If you are working towards being more spiritually in tune with yourself, you will need to find practices and routines that will work for you. There isn't a specific way to do things that will work for everyone, as this is going to be a journey where you will have to look at different things that will enable you to connect with your spirituality. Some suggestions are meditation, prayer, reading religious texts, going to your place of worship, connecting with others who have the same beliefs as you, and doing things to seek peace and enjoyment.

The Importance of Self-Care

There are so many people out there who are truly tired of being adults. It seems like it is filled with many responsibilities and problems and not nearly enough enjoyable moments. If you have not complained about this at some point, you probably have a few people around you who have. The problem is not with growing up or having these responsibilities, but because we are not focusing on our needs. Of course, you will not enjoy your life if you feel like your needs are not being met. This is why it is so easy to feel overwhelmed and stressed all the time. The solution to this is self-care.

When you decide to start taking care of yourself, you need to be deliberate about it. Otherwise, you run the risk of not doing it correctly and not getting the results you want. Self-care is essential because it causes you to develop and maintain a healthy relationship with yourself, which will allow you to put out good energy and feelings to the people around you. As a result, how you interact with others will change, and your happiness and satisfaction in life will no longer depend on others.

When you take the time to spend with yourself and truly take care of your needs, it benefits those around you as well. People who do not practice self-care can be grumpy, sad, and unable to create fulfilling interactions with the people around them, meaning that other people will not have pleasant interactions with you, and you will not be able to give your best to others. All of this will directly affect the people around you, so if you think it is selfish to practice self-care, think again. Everyone around you will also benefit from your self-care, even if they do not know it.

10 Ways to Take Better Care of Yourself

If you are struggling to think of ways to practice self-care, you can follow the tips laid out in this section. These things are the basics of self-care and will make you feel better about yourself and make your body feel better. You do not have to do all of these things at once since it can be overwhelming to try too many things at once. Instead, just pick a few and try them out. Once you have gotten used to the first few, you can add a few more into your routine.

Start Making Sleep Part of Your Selfcare Routine

Sleep plays such a big role in our lives, but most do not give it the attention it deserves. In fact, in extreme stress and anxiety seasons, the first thing we tend to give up is sleep. This is not healthy and has some very negative effects on you. Lack of sleep can cause health issues and make you feel low both physically and emotionally. Sleep is essential, and if there is any tip you take away from this section, it should be this one.

If you struggle with falling asleep at a decent hour or get restless, low-quality sleep when you fall asleep, you need to focus on creating an effective routine. Getting a good night's sleep is all about what you do before you put your head on that pillow. These are the things that will set you up for a healthy night's sleep, and they will lead to you feeling rested and rejuvenated in the morning.

The goal is not just that you can sleep for a long time, but that you have good-quality sleep as well. Many people think that a good night's rest is determined by the number of hours you are sleeping for, but it is not the most crucial thing while this is important. If you sleep for a total of eight hours but only have low-quality sleep where you have been tossing and turning the whole night, the amount of time you slept for is not going to matter. You will feel much more rested if you slept for six hours and had a peaceful and good quality sleep. Ideally, you should go for both length and quality. Our bodies need a specific amount of sleep at night, so you should aim for seven to nine hours per night. This will give your body time to rest and heal itself during the night. However, you will have to find the optimum amount of sleep for you within these parameters. Some people need less sleep, and others require a total of nine hours. You can test this by sleeping different lengths and seeing which one leaves you feeling the best when you wake up.

You should be preparing for your sleep about six to eight hours before you want to fall asleep. I know this might sound shocking, but let me explain. If you drink caffeine or have anything high in sugar too close to bedtime, you will struggle to fall asleep, as both give you energy. This can lead to you lying awake in your bed and tossing and turning during the night. You do not want to feel full of energy when you need to be falling asleep. While six to eight hours seems like a long time, it will give the body enough time to work out the caffeine and sugar in a way that will no longer affect your sleeping patterns. If you plan to go to bed at 10 pm, then you should stop taking in caffeine by 4 pm at the latest. You will find that you can fall asleep much easier, and your sleep will be a whole lot more restful.

The rest of your bedtime routine can be a whole lot closer to the time that you want to fall asleep, specifically about an hour to 30 minutes before you want to sleep. The main thing about your routine is that it has to be relaxing, and you should avoid anything that will spike up your energy levels. This means that you should not be doing exercise close to bedtime, and you should not be on your electronic devices. Training gives you a hit of energy and adrenaline, which will keep you up, so make sure that you exercise about three to four hours before bedtime if you work out in the evenings. Electronic devices emit blue light, which the body can mistake for sunlight. This means that the body will think it is daytime and will force you to stay awake. Put away all electronic devices, and do not look at them before bed. It is best to keep them off the bedside table as well, as it will be too easy to pick them up if you are lying in bed. Instead, leave it on the other side of the room. Another bonus is that you will have to get out of bed to switch off an alarm, which will stop you from hitting the snooze button.

Besides this, you can pretty much add anything you want to your nighttime routine, as long as it is relaxing. For example, you could try taking a bath, reading, doing a quick clean of your space, meditation, listening to a podcast, or preparing for the next day by taking out your clothes and writing out a to-do list. All of these things are low-energy tasks, meaning they will be ideal for getting ready for bed. You should do these things in the same order every night so that your body will start to recognize that you are starting your nighttime routine and it is getting close to bedtime. You will find that you start getting tired about halfway through the routine. This way, when you set your head on the pillow, you will have no trouble falling asleep.

Exercise and Movement

This is a great habit to have in your life because it promotes physical and mental well-being. If you are looking to better your physical and mental health, you must add this to your day. You don't have to do a hectic form of exercise to access its benefits, as simply choosing to move your body more is enough to feel better in every aspect. Our bodies were not designed to stay still for most of the day, but unfortunately, this is what most of us end up doing. We commute to work, sit at a desk for eight to nine hours, and then commute back. When we get home, we sit in front of the TV or do some other sedentary tasks. If your life looks similar to this, you need to add in some movement to your day.

Exercise is a great mood booster and stress reliever, which is why you should do it every day. You will need these benefits most days, and the great thing is that they stay with you for many hours after you have worked out. You should choose a form of exercise that you enjoy to be more likely to stick to it. The key is consistency, so pick something that you know you will want to keep up, and that will fit into your daily routine. Just 20 to 30 minutes of activity a day is enough to reap the benefits from it, so it isn't a lot of time going into it. I'm sure that you can find this time in some part of your day.

If you do not like the gym, you should choose from a whole host of other exercise options, such as going for a walk after dinner, riding a bike, participating in a sport like playing tennis, soccer, yoga, and joining an exercise class. Choose something that will work for you so that you know you will want to keep doing it. This should be a part of the day that you look forward to. While it may be hard to start, you will want to keep doing it once you notice how good you feel afterwards. Your body will feel better, and your mind will be calmer and more apparent.

Eat Healthily

The food we eat is supposed to nourish our bodies. However, it can be much easier to eat the quickest, most convenient thing around so that we can satisfy our hunger. This is because the foods we eat are crucial to our health and well-being, but eating unhealthy foods is a significant contributor to many physical and mental problems. For example, low energy, weight gain, and brain fog can stem from not eating the right foods to nourish the body.

It would be best if you were aiming to eat foods that will give your body the nutrients it needs. Just because a food is quick and tastes good does not mean you should eat it, as most foods that are available quickly are low in nutrients and are usually processed and filled with sugars. This includes take-out and junk food. Sure, they may taste great and be conveniently available, but this is the extent of their benefits to you. When you eat these kinds of foods, it can quickly affect your mood and energy levels. Remember that food is meant to fuel us for the day, so we need to be putting the right fuel into the body.

Whole foods are the best for the mind and body. These are the foods that have the most nutrients, and they will deliver what the body needs. Whole foods are in their most natural states, such as fruit, vegetables, and whole grains. Unprocessed meat also falls into this category. If you want to know how processed a food is, you just need to look at the food labels, and it will become evident. If the brand has lots of ingredients that look like they do not need to be there, then it is probably processed. The rule of thumb should be that you should not eat many foods that have ingredients that you cannot pronounce or have never heard of before, as that usually signifies that there are lots of preservatives and chemicals in that food. This is not something that you should be eating regularly.

However, this is not to say that you can never have take out or processed foods. The goal is not to eliminate these things but enjoy them in moderation. The bulk of your diet should be made up of whole foods, and you can enjoy the other foods as a treat now and then if you want to. You should also aim to make most of your meals at home since that lets you know what is going into it. You will also enjoy it more when you know that some work has gone into it. Cooking and preparing your meals is also a form of self-care, as it can be a time where your mind is wholly focused on what you are doing and not on other things in your life. Cooking can be a relaxing and enjoyable experience if you let it be.

The other aspect of eating healthy is to eat mindfully, which is when you are completely present when you are eating. Most people eat while doing other things; eating is not a priority but something that just needs to get done, so it is easier to choose fast foods over home-cooked meals. Eating should be an event that is separate from other activities. For example, rather than eating at your desk or watching a TV show, take the time to sit and enjoy your meal. Don't think about anything else besides enjoying your meal. This creates time for you to clear your mind and separate yourself from everything going on, making it an excellent time for a refresher during the day. You will also be able to listen to your body's hunger cues, meaning that you will be able to recognize when you are full and stop eating. It can be hard to acknowledge being full when you are busy, leading to overeating, feeling stuffed and sluggish. Finally, you don't have to take extensive time to eat. Just 20 minutes will be enough.

Take a Trip and Unplug

We all need a little break from our daily lives. It is a very healthy thing to do. If you take a step back, you will come back feeling rested and have a different perspective to deal with whatever you have to. We cannot just be in work mode all the time. You probably do get a few hours to relax in the day, and perhaps you have a relaxing weekend most of the time, but this is not enough. Sometimes, you need to unplug and reset completely. Step out of your routine and go somewhere else where you do not have responsibilities and commitments. We all need breaks like this because they refuel us and keep us going.

This trip does not have to be expensive, and it does not have to be something that you do every month. If you get away a couple of times a year, that will be enough. You can choose something local that doesn't cost too much. Just going away for a weekend is enough time to rejuvenate yourself. The goal when going away is to unplug and rest, which means that you should not be taking any work with you. I would even recommend that you limit your access to your phone. You are not obligated to answer calls or messages. This weekend is for you alone.

You can let the closest people to you know that you will be away and that you won't be answering all messages. If you have a spouse and kids, they can come with you; after all, family time is needed when you have a family. It can also help you relax, but if you do not want them to tag along, you should communicate this to them and make sure they understand where you're coming from.

Keep Track of Your Accomplishments

Life seems to keep pushing forward constantly, and it can be challenging to take the time to acknowledge what you have accomplished. So many people out there feel like they are not where they should be in life and have not accomplished enough. It is not that they have not accomplished enough, but that they do not take the time to acknowledge them. Wherever you accomplish something, you need to take note of it and celebrate. This will make your life feel fulfilling because you will see that you're moving forward.

To take this a step further, you should note all of your accomplishments in the day. Each day needs to be celebrated, and you would be surprised at how much you got done when you look at it properly. Most of us move from one task to the next without even thinking about it, then feel sad or disappointed at the end of the day because we think we have not done enough. It is essential to spend some time to recap the day and see what you have accomplished. It doesn't matter if the tasks were huge, or if they were tiny because simple things like washing the dishes and organizing your desk need to be celebrated too. You will find that you become more appreciative of where you are in life as you do this more, and you will be more present in your day.

Spend Time Being Grateful

There has been a movement of people starting to keep gratitude journals and filling them every day. This is a fantastic habit because gratitude is a forgotten trait that has many benefits for you. When we are grateful for what we have, we enjoy our lives much more, as it puts things in perspective and helps us see that we have a lot to be thankful for. It can be so easy to get caught up in the negative aspects of life and then hyper focus on them, but when we do this all the time, we can send ourselves into a negative spiral. It is incredibly difficult to enjoy your life if you only see the negatives in it. Nobody has a perfect life, so we all have the choice about what we focus on. If you want to live a happier, more positive, and more mentally healthy life, then you should choose to look at the positives.

The best thing to do is keep a journal to save a note of everything you are grateful for. You can write in it at the end of the day when you are about to go to bed, then look back on your day and list things you are grateful for. Even if they are small things, they are worth putting down. You could be thankful for your house, family, job; today's alright traffic, the stranger who smiled at you, and anything else that added to your day. If you are ever feeling low, you can look back on your journal and see how many things you must be thankful for.

It would help to let others know when you are grateful for things, they have done for you. Showing gratitude to others will help you strengthen your relationships. Everyone likes to feel valued and appreciated. If you are the one that offers this to them, people will want to do more for you and will want to be around you. The great thing about this is that other people will often reciprocate what they have received, so people will be more open to showing gratitude for you when you have already done this for them. It opens up a whole new line of communication. When people appreciate you, it is a definite mood booster.

Create an Inspiring or Cozy Space

We all need a space in our homes where we can escape, where we can unwind or get creative if we need to. This can be a bedroom, study, garage, or any other room that you love being in. It depends on your personality and what you want the room to be to you. Whatever you choose, you should aim to have a safe space that you can call your own.

Even if it is not a whole room, it could be a corner of a room you love sitting in. The point is to have some sort of escape and a place that you feel relaxed in or inspire you.

Besides having the free space to go to, decorating, designing, and preparing can be a great way to self-care. There is something about working in a room or an area that makes you feel good. When you see the end result, you will be incredibly proud of yourself. You can do whatever you want in the space, such as repaint, add some new furniture, DIY a few things for the room, and design it any other way you want it. If you find joy doing these first of things, then you can keep re-doing the room and others in your home. This is a great activity to spend some time with yourself and forget about everything else for a moment.

Create Something New

There is something about creating something so refreshing and fun. We were all about making things, from mudpies to macaroni necklaces and drawings, when we were kids. It didn't matter because all we wanted to do was get our hands dirty and create something. This might start seeming a bit silly as we get older since we have other more "important" things to do, but I think that it is worth going back to our inner child and finding joy in making something new.

You could have a specific talent for making things, or you could be a complete novice. Your skill doesn't matter here, but what does matter is that you just try and see where it goes. You never know whether you will be really good at whatever you choose to do. It might lead you to your new hobby. Woodwork, painting, drawing, cooking, and backing are all great options. As I said, it doesn't matter what you make or how good you are at it. The point is that you try to create something. When you are done, you will feel a sense of pride in yourself, which is the point of creating something. If you are good at it and have a talent for it, you can continue with it. Even if you do not have a natural talent, you should continue if you enjoy doing whatever it is. It is not about showing off to other people but finding enjoyment in the creation process. Who knows? Perhaps you will get better and improve your skills along the way.

Go Outside

The outdoors is a great place to be. We all need a little fresh air and sunlight each day since it helps us reduce our stress and lower blood pressure. It can also help you feel more awake, full of energy and improve your mood. This has a lot of benefits from just taking a step out the door. The fresh air really will do you some good, and you will feel so much better when you come back inside.

Most of us spend a majority of our lives indoors, under artificial light. It is not healthy to just stay stuck inside. It can lead to depressed feelings. We all need to take some time each day to be outside and breathe in some fresh air. It is even better if you can get to a place that has some natural plants around, as the greenery is beneficial to your mood and just really lovely to look at. You don't have to do anything while you are outside; just sitting and enjoying the sun on your face and the wind in your hair is enough. You should aim to get at least 20 minutes of outdoor time a day. You will feel that your mood improves and that you feel a lot calmer when you do this.

Schedule Your Self-Care Time

It can be hard to find some extra time for yourself during the day. We are all busy, and sometimes it can just slip the mind. This is why it is important to schedule it into your day. You should have a designated time where you just focus on yourself. This is where you take the time to make yourself the priority. You can do whatever you want in this time as long as you find it relaxing and fulfilling. You could work on a hobby, take a nap, take a bath, go for a walk, or do anything else that you want to do. There are no rules here, as long as you do not compromise this time with yourself. It doesn't even have to be an extensive amount of time. 30 minutes will be enough time to just do whatever you want.

Chapter 4:

Is Self-Care Selfish?

Many people think that self-care is selfish. This is a common myth, and it is time to dispel it. A group of people will use self-care as an excuse to be selfish, but that is not what it is about. Self-care is not about just thinking about yourself to a point where you stop caring about the well-being of others and is the opposite. You can care for yourself and others simultaneously, but you just need to know how to strike a balance. There is a line separating self-care and selfishness, and we will discuss all of that in this chapter.

The Difference Between Self-Care and Selfishness

If you have ever thought of self-care and thought it was a selfish act, then you have been taught the wrong version of self-care. Unfortunately, some people misuse self-care. People believe that self-care is an excuse or a bad thing. I want to reassure you that self-care is not about being so focused on yourself that you lose sight of others. All the tips and points discussed in the previous chapters have never alluded to you being selfish in a way that will negatively affect those you love.

With that out of the way, let's dig a little deeper into what these two things are so that you can see that there is a definite distinction between them. Self-care is making yourself better to interact with others and not project your feelings and issues on others. When we do not take care of ourselves, it can be easy to pile our problems on others. It is not healthy for us or those we are projecting on, as it saddles them with an extra burden they did not ask for and might not be able to handle.

When you choose self-care, you choose to live up to your full potential and discover your purpose. This is something that will be forced on you, but it is not selfish by any means. What you are doing is trying to find your place in society and seeing what makes you happy. We all have a space to take up in society. If we can discover where we belong, we will be able to operate in our positions to the best of our abilities, contributing more to society and others. This does benefit you, but it also benefits others both directly and indirectly.

Selfishness, on the other hand, is all about having a me-focused mentality. This is where you are only thinking of your own needs and how to meet them, even if it is at the expense of others. Often selfish people are so focused on themselves that they cannot build fulfilling relationships with others. The relationships they do have serve the purpose of meeting one of their needs and advancing their agendas. Selfish people do not consider other people's feelings when they do things. When someone is selfish, they will not have many people around them because nobody likes to be around a selfish person.

The main difference between the two is the motive behind the actions. You can perform the same action for a selfish reason or for one that is focused on self-care. For example, you could decline to help someone because you don't want to and it has no benefit to you, or because you have to take some time for yourself or do not have the time to take on a new task. The first set of reasons are selfish because they have no regard for the other person and are only thinking about themselves. The second set of reasons is for self-care reasons, where you know that you will not be able to give your all to the task, and it would be better for the both of you if the other person found someone else to help them. Remember that self-care is done with the intention of taking care of yourself, not about taking away from others or harming them.

Why Self-Care is Not Selfish

Self-care is beneficial for everyone in your life. It might seem like an odd statement, but it is a true one. When you are fully taken care of, you can give to others. Self-care makes you a better parent, spouse, friend, colleague, sibling, and child. It makes us better people and helps us reach our full potential, which will spill over into others. When you are more in touch with your needs, you can show a deeper empathy towards people and have a lot more in your heart to help them when needed. People who do not take the time to take care of themselves will be less effective because they can burn out really quickly. You can't just drive a car endlessly on one tank of gas, after all, because it will eventually run out, and you won't be able to go anywhere. You have to take the time to stop and fill up the tank before the car can meet your needs. This is how we all work as well. You have to be filled up first before you can be of any use to others.

When you feel that you have been adequately cared for, you will be more open to giving to others. Think back to times where you had felt drained, and it just felt like everything has been taken from you. If your child was going to come to you and ask for something, the chances are that you would think of it as another inconvenience to your day and would not want to do it. You do not wish to listen to your spouse and support them if needed. You do not want to help a colleague with a problem they are having. This is all because you have no more patience left, and your tank has been left empty. If you want to help these people and have fulfilling relationships, then self-care is necessary.

Self-care is also not selfish because the aim is not to take from others. Selfish people do not mind taking from others because they only care about what will benefit them. On the other hand, someone choosing self-care is doing something for themselves without taking it from others. The only way you will be taking from someone is if you have committed to them and break it and leave them with a problem. In chapter two, we spoke about saying no. If you do this, other people will not rely on you when you cannot deliver. In this way, you are not selfish because you were honest, and while it might seem disappointing to them at the moment, this is better for them in the long term.

We need to step out of the mindset that doing something for ourselves is selfish. There is no way that we can just keep doing things for others and never stop thinking of ourselves. This is an unsustainable way to live, and I would not recommend it to anyone. You don't have to think about others constantly; it is okay to think of yourself and choose things that will make you happy. You also don't have to feel like you must justify all of your actions. You know when you are selfish and when you really just need some time for yourself. Self-care is not selfish when you know that you are going to come back when your tank is full, giving the people around you a better version of yourself.

Why Do People Think Self-Care is Selfish?

People tend to think that anyone who focuses on themselves is a selfish person, even though the end goal of self-care is to come back with positive energy that you can put back into the world. I would also say that people who think self-care is selfish are selfish themselves. When you take a step back to focus on yourself, it might inconvenience someone else, especially if you have always been there when they needed you. However, if this is the person telling you that you are selfish, I would check their motives. This might be a way to make you feel guilty for not being there for them, which is the antithesis of being selfish.

The majority of people who would label self-care as selfish are selfish people themselves. You need to be careful when dealing with people like this because they are not in it for others and are looking for the most beneficial. Most people will think that taking time for yourself is being selfish if it results in them doing extra work. Remember that you do not have a responsibility to make another person's life easier. You can help out if you can, but all of it should not fall onto you. Just be careful when you're dealing with people who call you selfish. If it is not a close friend or family member, or someone else you trust, you might be facing a manipulative person who is in it for their gain. You know your motives and your needs, and nobody has the right to make you feel guilty for doing something for yourself.

Chapter 5:

Breaking Free From the Constraint of Helping Others Before Yourself

It can be easy to fall into a pattern of taking care of others and not ourselves. This can happen for many reasons, and most of the time, we do not even know what we are doing. If you are the type of person constantly giving to others, you need to step back and see if this is harming you. As stated before, taking care of yourself is your priority, and everything else should follow.

Possible Reasons You Are Helping Others Instead of Yourself

There are many reasons why you are helping others instead of yourself first, and it is crucial to get down to the root cause of this so that you can fix the problem. These sorts of things must be dealt with at the root of it all. Otherwise, you will just be doing a surface-level fix, which is ultimately not sustainable. As you read through the following, I want you to think back on your relationships and interactions with others and see if you can find any similarities. Think about your thought patterns and dig a little deeper to identify the cause and mental root.

They Remind You of Someone in Your Past

The types of people we were exposed to are often those we find ourselves subconsciously attracted to. Even if that person is not good, we are used to that type of behaviour and are more likely to stick around for it. For example, people with verbally and emotionally manipulative parents tend to have relationships with people who share these characteristics. People who have a healthier home life would choose to be in relationships with people who mirror what they have already experienced in their lives. This is not a hard and fast rule, but there is definitely a correlation between our past relationships and the people we choose to have relationships within the present. This is why we see that people tend to marry those who remind them of their parents in terms of behavior.

This is a completely subconscious thing because we are attracted to familiar things, which gives us a sense of comfort even if the person is unhealthy. The comfort comes from knowing what to expect. If you have had people in your past who have taken advantage of you and whom you were always sacrificing for, then this might be the reason you are doing it now as well. This creates an unhealthy cycle of relationships that can be difficult to get out of, which is why it is important to deal with your past before you step into new relationships. I would suggest seeking closure and perhaps even counseling to help you to close the door to unhealthy relationships. You do not have to be defined by what you did in the past, and it is best to be conscious of it to avoid it in the present.

If you can see similar patterns in your relationships today that you dealt with in the past, this is an indication that you are stuck in a bad relationship cycle. You can break this by looking back on your past and digging deeper into those relationships. It helps to write down and acknowledge all the negative aspects of the relationships back then. The goal is to not find yourself in relationships with people who are going to use you again. You can use your past relationships to help you identify the red flags you should be looking out for, and once you have done so, you can try and avoid these things as best you can. Remember, you do not have to be in a relationship with anyone you feel will be unhealthy for you. You have the power to choose your relationships, so choose them wisely.

You Confuse Rescuing With Caring

One of the most common reasons people skip out of self-care is trying to rescue everyone else. If you are constantly trying to help and fix everyone else's problems, you will not have time for yourself. The thing is that people need to be able to learn their own life lessons, even if that means that they fail a few times. We do not like to see the people we love go through hard times or fail, but it is often necessary for their own personal growth. Constantly swooping in to save people hinders their development and does not allow them to grow up and learn how to deal with their own problems. If you are always there for them, they will never be able to stand up on their own two feet.

Rescuing people is selfish. Being there too much for someone is an act of selfishness because you decide how their life should play out, and they cannot take complete control. While it might seem that they like you to be there for them all the time, this will usually lead to resentment down the line or to that person being lazy and incapable of doing things without you. There is no way that you will always be there for that person. One day, you will not be there for them, and then they will have to do everything by themselves and be stuck with a considerable disadvantage. We see overbearing parents do this to their children. When the kids grow up, they either try and get as far away from their parents as possible, or they stick so closely to their parents that they cannot make a success of their own lives.

The best way to help others is to focus on ourselves and allow them to focus on themselves. While we think that reducing people's unpleasant things in their lives is a selfless act, we must look at its motives and realise that we are holding our loved ones back. It can be a hard truth to face because we genuinely think that we are doing this in the best interest of our loved ones, but it also causes you to carry the burden of stress for the other person. You not only have to worry about your life but the life of the other person. This is not sustainable, and it will inevitably become too much to handle. This is often where resentment sets in, and that is not a place you want to be with any person you love.

The important thing here is understanding the difference between providing support and taking action on the other person's behalf. Other people do not need rescuing and saving. It is okay to let the ones you love go through things and build their own lives up. If you have always been the type to try and fix others, this will be incredibly hard to stop doing. You will have to force yourself to take a step back. If the person is used to you taking care of them all the time, this will be hard for them, and they might even be upset by it. You should explain your reasoning for taking a step back and do your best to have an open conversation with them. This will hopefully make it easier for both of you. If the other person tries to guilt you for taking a step back, you will need to stand up for yourself and stand firm in your decision. What may be hard in the present will be completely worth it down the line.

You Have Gotten Used to Relationships Based on Needs and Not Real Love

Neediness is often mistaken for love. Someone who needs you all the time can make you feel wanted, and being there for that person can be a form of loving them. The problem is that love and being needed are not the same thing. One of the things that are to blame for this misrepresentation is the media. We watch these movies about people needing each other to be complete and then doing everything together. It is no wonder there are so many people who have this skewed version of love in their heads. This is not true love, and it is definitely not sustainable.

This view on relationships leads us to give too much of ourselves to the other person. This can be in romantic relationships, familial relationships and any other kind of relationship you have. Relationships are not there to make you feel good about yourself or meet your needs, and they are also not there for you to meet someone else's needs or make the other person feel good about themselves. Relationships are supposed to be give-and-take, so your relationship is not healthy if this is not happening.

We are responsible for our own health, well-being and meeting our own needs. Nobody can do that for us, and that means that we should not do that for others. While it might sound incredible just to pour yourself into someone, it is a trap that can later lead to resentment in the relationship. It is not a sustainable way to live for you or the other person. You cannot love someone so much that you forget that you are also important. You also need to take care of your needs, and you won't have enough energy to do so if you are always focused on the other person.

When you are able to focus on yourself and take care of your needs, your other relationships will be better for it. You will be able to give from a palace of wholeness, and you will not have to try so hard all the time. The relationship will be pure and natural, which is the best kind of relationship. It would help if you focused on working on yourself independently from your partner or other all-consuming relationship so that you will be so much better for each other when you are together.

You Expect the Same From Others

When we are helping others, we often like to believe that we are doing so for unselfish reasons, but the truth might be vastly different. The truth is that we sometimes do this because we are expecting something in return and that we are constantly helping people because we want the same thing from them. You know that your motives are not entirely pure when you are in need, and others don't come to your aid, and your immediate reaction is to be hurt, angry, or disappointed.

The thing is that people do not owe you anything. The same is true for you, however, because you do not owe anyone anything. If you choose to do something for someone else, that does not guarantee that they will be there for you. In fact, you are just teaching people how to treat you in most cases. If you portray yourself as a rescuer and the one that will jump in to help, then this is how people will look at you. Whenever they need someone, they will quickly call you because they know you will be there. However, this does not mean that you will be able to call them.

People can take advantage of your caring nature because they know that you will just do things for them. This may not be done with malicious intent, but it is harmful to you either way, which is why you need to have boundaries when it comes to helping people. You can only give so much, and it is not okay for you to be putting yourself last so that you can cater to everyone else. You need to know that people often won't reciprocate. Taking care of yourself is your priority, just like how other people are responsible for taking care of themselves.

You Are Focusing More on the Goal Than the Person

When you are emotionally attached to a person, you can start to focus on their needs all the time. This happens more if you're an emotionally driven person. You want the other person to be successful and reach their full potential. This is a fantastic thing, but it will be very bad for you and your relationship if it is powered in the wrong way. What can happen is that you can get pushy and try so hard to make the other person's goals happen for them that negative outcomes occur.

Emotional people care deeply for others, and they have a deep sense of compassion because they feel what others are feeling. This is an excellent thing because you can truly empathise with others, and other people will feel safe with you, but the downside of this is that you can start taking too much control over the other person's life. For example, if you care deeply about a person, you will also care deeply about their dreams and goals. This could cause you to keep getting involved and start doing things that the other person should be doing on their own. This is where you need to take a step back and realize that your emotions are driving you to prioritize the other person over yourself. We cannot take care of both ourselves and another person entirely.

If you keep giving, it can make you feel resentful because it might seem like you are putting in more effort for the other person than themselves. People get lazy when there is too much help offered to them. If someone offered to do all your homework when you were in school, I'm sure you would have said yes because it was easier for someone else to do it than for you to put in the work. However, you will have to face the consequences for this later on when you start getting bad marks in school because you do not know your work. While helping the person might seem reasonable in the short term, it might be detrimental to them later down the line. If you care about the other person, the best thing you can do for them is let them take action for their own dreams and goals.

It can be easy to just focus on the future happiness that will take place when this person reaches their goals, but you have to look at what is happening now. You can support the other person as they are trying to achieve their goals. Be there for them, talk to them, and give them advice if needed, but don't do the work for them. The end goal is not yours to reach. It is their journey, and they must do it on their own. You should have your own goals that you work towards. Refocus that energy onto yourself, and push for your dreams and goals.

You Don't Realize Your Worth

The harsh reality for many people is that they do not think of themselves as necessary compared to other people in their lives, so they pour themselves into others instead of focusing on themselves. Therefore, if you believe that you are worthless to other people, they will start thinking about it, which will lead to you being taken advantage of.

When we are confident in ourselves and truly love ourselves, we will respect ourselves enough not to let others' needs eclipse our own. You are your first priority, and any lies in your head telling you otherwise need to be stopped. You decide the value you have in life. If you think highly of yourself, then so will others. Suppose you look at people who are in really high positions in companies. In that case, they have confidence in themselves, and you would never see someone asking them to do something menial or that would inconvenience them. You can have that same confidence, and all you have to do is know your worth. We are going to talk more about this so that you know how to tap into your confidence.

How to Improve Your Confidence and Self-Worth

People who have a high level of confidence and know what they are worth are the people who are respected. These people take care of themselves because they know they are worth it, and they won't do things for others if it isn't worth their time to do so. While there is a risk of being overly confident, you still need some level of confidence to focus on yourself and give attention to the things that are important to you. If you are constantly saying yes to people and not prioritizing yourself, there is a good chance that you don't have a lot of confidence and self-esteem. Thankfully, these are things that can be worked on. We will go through a few things that you can do to improve the way you look at yourself, which will let you see how valuable you are.

Identify and Change Your Negative Beliefs

Our self-worth and confidence stem from what we think about ourselves. If we look down on ourselves, then we will feel like we are worthless. The key is to identify these thought patterns and change them. Most people will have some negative thoughts about themselves at some point since we are our own worst critics. It is actually pretty normal to have some bad thoughts about yourself in isolated incidents. This is usually due to something not going our way, failing at something, or something that has played on our insecurities. Passing thoughts are something that most of us will deal with. Most of the time, this is manageable, and the thoughts will go away. The problem comes when these become the default thoughts, and patterns start arising. If you are always thinking negative things about yourself, then it is time to make some changes.

The first thing that you need to do is to recognize the thought in the moment. Once you do, you can then focus on changing the view. This is something that you will have to work towards. It will take some time to change your thought patterns, but it is possible. As soon as a negative thought pops into your head, you need to look for evidence that supports it, and there will often be no evidence that will support negative thinking about yourself. These thoughts have no factual basis, which makes them easy to dispel. For example, if the view is, "I am such a horrible friend," ask yourself why you think so, then look for something in your life that will prove this wrong. Think of all the good things you have done for your friends that show you are a good friend. It would also help if you wrote down the thought and the statement that makes the belief false. The more you do this, the more you will get used to dispel these thoughts. Eventually, you will be able to let the thoughts pass through without even being affected by them. Hopefully, you will stop thinking these thoughts altogether.

Notice the Positive Things About Yourself

When we do not have high self-esteem, it can be challenging to see the positives in ourselves. But, when we see that many things about ourselves are positives, it will improve how we think about ourselves and increase our confidence. If you have never done this before, it might seem strange and a little bit difficult in the beginning. But, as you keep noticing the positives, you will get better at it, and the way you look at yourself will improve as well.

A good practice to get into is to write down all the positive things about yourself. You can spend some time in the morning thinking about a few positive things and write them down. Then, you can look at them whenever you have some negative thoughts about yourself. It will also bolster your confidence when you have already thought about things you like about yourself. It is the tiny things that matter. We all have some good things about ourselves, but the challenge is to bring those things to the forefront of our minds. This will also help you kick out the negative thoughts that might try and creep in now and then.

Start Saying What You Want to Believe

Words have immense power, so we need to watch what we say to ourselves. If we are speaking negatively to ourselves, then these emotions are what will be manifested. On the other hand, if we have positive and uplifting things to say to ourselves, on the other hand, then we will see the result of this in our lives. Therefore, you have to start positively talking to yourself. One way you can do this is by having affirmation that you repeat to yourself.

Many very successful people have affirmations that they say to themselves. This helps them feel more confident in themselves. It allows them to see how important they are in their operational areas. Affirmations are usually very personal because you know what you need to hear. If you need to be more confident, then you need to tell yourself that you're confident. If you want to have more self-esteem, you need to say how important you are. The more you say it, the more you will believe it.

Start Taking On Challenges

When you have low self-esteem, you shy away from challenges because you do not believe that you can do them. This is probably something we have all struggled with in the past. It is essential that we take on challenges even when we do not feel like it. You are better than you give yourself credit for, and this means that you have far more potential than you know. Most of the time, we do not accept challenges because we think they will be too complex and fail. While this might happen, it is not something to be scared of. Even if you do fail, you would have learned something from it, so it will never be a total loss.

Challenges are designed to help us learn and grow, making us better because we are forced to push ourselves past our perceived limits. The more challenges we take on, the more confident we become, and we start thinking that we will beat a challenge before we even do it. This is the kind of confidence you need to keep you going so that you may see your worth.

It feels so good to take on something hard and actually be able to do it. You will be a better person at the end of a challenge than you were when you began. This is the beauty of challenges. We are all capable of becoming so much more than what we are right now. We just have to be willing to take on the challenges that will get us there.

Perhaps there are no challenging situations that you can put yourself in right now. In this case, you need to make your own challenges. There are challenges all over, and we just have to look for them. A challenge will be something that you have never done before or that you are scared of doing. This could be something small like trying new food, walking up to a stranger and talking to them, or trying a new hobby. It could also be something quite big and scary, like bungee jumping, getting a tattoo, or asking your boss for that promotion. Challenges can be anything that will break the mold of what you think of yourself right now.

I can tell you from experience that we shy away from challenges because we are scared of a negative outcome. However, I can also tell you that negative outcomes are never as bad as we think they will be. They are never world-shattering or so embarrassing that you cannot recover from it. The negative outcome is not even negative in most cases; if you ask your boss for a promotion and they say no, you have not lost anything. However, there is the potential that your boss will keep an eye on you because they know that you are looking for advancement, so you might be the first person on their mind when an opportunity does arise. A small negative experience like your boss saying no) leads to a potentially positive experience, such as the opportunity to be noticed for another position.

I challenge you to take up a challenge, even if you have to start small and build your way up. It's essential to try something new every week to challenge yourself and grow in your capacity constantly. You will feel more confident when you do this, and you will also increase your skillset. There are many positives to taking on new challenges, so don't shy away from them. This is one of the best things you can do for yourself, and it can be a form of self-care because you are doing things that are focused on improving yourself.

Learn to Accept Compliments

How many times have you turned down a compliment? My guess is quite a few times. Most of us do this all the time. When someone compliments us, we tend to disagree with them and put down the compliment. This is usually in an effort to be humble, or so we have been taught. I don't think that there is any good that comes from turning down a compliment. There is no person out there who compliments someone and thinks, "I hope they disagree with the compliment I am about to give them." People compliment each other when they genuinely like or admire something about the other person. They want to express these feelings, and that is perfectly normal.

When someone compliments you, all you have to do is say thank you. You don't have to expand on it or say anything else. A simple thank you is more than enough, and it is not a hard thing to do. If you have any urges to put yourself down at this moment, you have to resist them. Complements are gratifying experiences when you allow them to be because you get to see that other people notice good things about you while they see the positives in you and feel the need to express them. This is a fantastic thing. If someone else notices something good about you, it must be true, and it is okay to enjoy the compliment.

Some people feel like they are being conceded when they accept a compliment, but this is not true. You are not searching for this complement. If someone else feels the need to say something nice about you, this is not you being full of yourself. If you let compliments in, they have the power to make you feel good about yourself and bolster your confidence.

When you have low self-esteem, compliments can make you feel awkward. If you think this way, you will need to push through this feeling and resist the urge to bat away the complaint. Like I mentioned earlier, all you need to say is thank you. You do not need to elaborate on it, and you don't even have to complement the other person back. The goal, in the beginning, is to learn just to let the compliments be. Eventually, you will not feel that you need to hide from compliments, and they will become a normal part of your life. Once that starts happening, you will enjoy getting compliments. This is a great space to be in because you will appreciate that others appreciate certain things about you. You will quickly find that you feel much better about yourself and that your confidence increases.

Take Care of Yourself

Many people do not prioritize self-care because they do not think they are worth it. In most cases, the best way to break this thought pattern is to start taking care of yourself, even if you do not feel like you are worth it. The more you prioritize yourself, the more you will see that you have value, which will eventually make you want to care for yourself even more. It is almost a cycle, but you have to jump in somewhere. If you cannot mentally realize that you are worth it, you need to start by doing something physical so that your mind catches up.

We only ever take care of things that we find valuable, which is a mental shift when you start taking care of yourself. The more you start taking care of something, the more value it will have to you. For example, two people can have the exact same car, but that vehicle will mean much more to the person who spends time working on it and taking care of it. That person will be proud of the car and will want to show it off. This is because when you take care of something, you form a connection to it. You put work into it, and this adds to its value. This is what you have to do for yourself. You need to start taking care of yourself so that your value in your mind starts to increase.

Chapter 6:

Help! I Am Addicted to Solving

Other People's Problems

Helping people seems like a strange addiction because it doesn't seem as bad as other addictions that people struggle with. However, I am going to disagree with this statement. Any addiction can be harmful because it is done in excess, and moderation is the key to balance and health. Additionally, a habit is something that you compulsively keep doing even if you know that it can be bad for you. The reason you keep doing it is that it offers some reward. The reward might not be obvious, but there must be one for you to keep doing something. Perhaps you like the way helping others makes you feel, or you hope that the reward for helping someone will be that they will become closer to you. Whatever it is, you need to move away from compulsively assisting people so that you can move forward in life.

Why Am I Drawn to Fixing Other People's Problems?

People who are natural caregivers have a higher tendency to want to help people than people who are not. Being a caregiver is perfect because you care for people and want to see them succeed. However, if this goes a bit overboard, you could forget about taking care of yourself. Natural caregivers must also remember that they have needs that need to be cared for and that caring for people does not have to be a relentless string of sacrifices. While being a natural caregiver might be a big reason you like to solve other people's problems, there are a few others. Let's go through them and see if you identify with any of them.

We Have a Need For Control

One of the most common reasons we may have an obsession with fixing other people's problems is that we have a control issue. If this is the case, we often force ourselves into situations in which we don't belong. People might not even ask for assistance most of the time, but you give it to them anyway because you want to control the outcome.

This is a subconscious thing, so you may not know that you are doing it, and you might even convince yourself that you are an excellent friend or partner for getting involved.

Let's take a look at an example to illustrate this better. Let's say that your friend is having a tough time at work. They are not enjoying the work they are doing, and their boss is grating on their nerves. Every time they vent, you say things like, "Are you looking for something else?" "You need to just leave!" or "There are other opportunities. You need to take it." These all might sound like great advice, but they show that you want to take control of the situation. If the other person does not ask for your advice, then they probably do not need it. When people tell you about their problems, they are often looking to vent and let it out. In this case, your friend probably knows that they should look for something else. If they are not, then maybe they do not want to and are just frustrated.

You might even take it a step further by searching for other jobs for them and then sending it through to them. You might also see if you have any contacts that could help. In the proper context, these are all great things to do for someone. The thing is, if they have not asked you to help them, all of this is intrusive. It is an attempt to say that you know better than them and are trying to lead them. You do not know their job the way they do, so most of the things you are doing are likely irrelevant. There is a line that is being crossed.

The truth is that the other person's job problems have nothing to do with us. Why do you feel so involved, then? It is because this problem makes you feel uncomfortable. After all, things are uncertain. If you love to be in control, any uncertainty will make you feel uncomfortable, even when it happens to others. So, when looking for a solution, you seek a way to make yourself feel better and not help the other person solve their problems. This is not helpful. Help is when you help them find solutions, not when you shove ideas down their throat, hoping they will take it.

If hearing about the job problem makes you feel uncomfortable and can't help yourself from trying to solve the problem, you need to have a conversation with your friend. People who like to have control are not bad. It is suitable for your own goals and dreams because you will go after what you want. However, if you distract yourself from doing this by fixing other people's problems, it won't be good for both of you. One of the best things you can do to help keep your impulses at bay is to ask the person before they start venting if they are looking for advice/help or want to vent. This will help you react to the situation appropriately.

They probably want to vent in most cases, so you know that you should not take any action. However, suppose you cannot stand listening to the venting because no action is taken to change the situation. In that case, you should be honest with them and say that you would prefer not to hear about this situation again and suggest that you talk about something else. This might be hard to do, but it will save both of you in the long run.

We Feel That We Are Responsible For Others' Happiness

When we try to fix other people's problems, we often feel responsible for their happiness. The truth is that you do not have any responsibility for other people's happiness. Everyone is in charge of their own happiness. Trying to shoulder another person's happiness and yours simultaneously is too heavy a burden to carry, and it will eventually lead to burnout. If a person wants to be happy, they need to chase after it themselves. There is nothing that you can do that will get them there sooner.

This has nothing to do with being there for the person and helping them through any tough times. This is something that you can do all while having clear boundaries in place. You are not the ONLY person that can help them. They have control over their situations, and they can find their happiness without your intervention.

We Are Not Truly Listening

Often, when people vent about their problems, they are not looking for a solution. They want to get out all of their frustrations. Venting is not an invitation for you to do something. In most cases, they are just looking for a sounding board and some emotional support. It is easy to tell the difference between someone looking for help and someone just looking to vent. A person that wants help and advice will ask for it. They will say, "What do you think I should do?". "I could use some advice.", "Could you help me with this?" or something along those lines. Someone who is just looking to vent will probably just rattle off about their problems.

If your first response to someone's venting is to give them advice or try to solve the problem, then you are not listening to what they have to say. When someone is venting, your job is only to engage in the conversation. The person will ask for your advice if they need it, but if they don't, then you can just leave it as it is. Be present in the conversation, and don't run through ways to solve the problem in your head. Just listen. This will be hard for you if you are a fixer, but you will get better at it as you practice.

Fixing Other Problems Leaves Us With a Low Opinion of Them

When we constantly try to fix other people's problems, we subconsciously think they cannot help themselves. This contributes to us having a low opinion of them. It is almost like thinking that person is not content enough to handle their own life. Adults should be able to solve their problems and take situations that happen in their life. When you are constantly willing to bail someone out, give them money, or pull together other parts of their lives, you say that they cannot handle their own lives.

We take care of children because they do not have the ability to take care of themselves. We buy them stuff, feed them, give them money when they need it, and sometimes we even get involved in fixing their mistakes. We do this because we know that they cannot do it on their own. They do not have the ability or life experience to do these things independently because they are just kids. When it comes to adults, however, we can't treat them the same way. Babying an adult is demeaning and something we should avoid at all costs.

This is also bad for us and our relationship with them. If we keep coming to their aid, even when they do not ask for it, we inhibit our ability to respond to situations correctly. Instead, we think about fixing the problem instead of actively being part of a productive conversation. You will also end up internalizing other people's problems as your own, which is unhealthy because you have your own issues to deal with that are now being left on the backburner.

Fixing Other Problems Appears to Be Easier Than Your Problems

This one might be a tough pill to swallow if you fall into this category, but if you can recognize it and make the right changes, you will be able to come out on the other side as a much better person. Focusing on fixing other people's problems could be an escape for you. When you compare other people's issues to yours, it can seem that they are easier to fix. If you are trying to ignore your problems, it would be easier to focus on someone else's problems.

Their problems may not be more accessible; it just looks like they are because you are not fully involved. There is less on the line for you if something goes wrong or the plan doesn't work. If you try and help someone else with an issue at work and it doesn't work out, you won't be the one that gets in trouble and whose job is one the line. However, if you do something wrong at your job, you will be the one who has to face the full force of the consequences.

If you are trying to escape your problems by fixing other people's problems, it needs to stop immediately. This is a horrible pattern to fall into because you are running away from the things that you need to deal with. You are the only person in charge of your life, which means that you are the only person who can fix it or make the changes needed. Building the life that you want is possible, but it takes work.

If you find yourself in this category of people, you first need to look at all the "projects" you are helping with for other people. Then, you need to go to those people and let them know that you will no longer support them because you have a whole lot to deal with in your own life, and you cannot do everything. If you cannot do this, you can still fulfill your commitments, but make sure you do not agree to anything else. This is a great time to practice what you learnt in chapter two and learn how to say no.

Once you are free from all other commitments, you will need to give your full attention to your life. Take out a pen and paper and make a list of all you need to deal with. If you have been running away for a while, there might be quite a bit that you have to deal with, so you could ask a close friend or family member to help sort through everything. Once you have a list of all the things that you need to take care of in your life, you need to tackle them one at a time. You can pick the most urgent things first and then keep going until you have dealt with everything. Make sure that you list everything, from financial commitments to relational commitments that you have been neglecting. You will feel so much lighter and in control once you have gotten a handle on everything. From here, you just need to make sure that you do not fall back into this pattern.

Chapter 7:

You Are Allowed to Help People

After everything we have spoken about, you might get the idea that you should stay away from helping people, but this is not the case. You can help people and offer yourself services to them, but it has to be under the right circumstances. Until now, we have been speaking about how important it is to take care of yourself. This chapter will go through how you can assist others and be there for them, all while not compromising all the progress you have made with your self-care.

Help Individuals With Things That are Simple for You

When you start helping people out, you need to be sure that you can offer a valuable service to them. Sometimes, you will just not be the right person to do the job or for them to talk to. This is perfectly fine, but make sure that you do not pretend that you have all the answers and can help them with something you do not have experience with. For example, if someone asks for advice or help with something you are uncomfortable with, you can tell them just that. This will save both of you time, and the person can go and find someone who will be more suitable to help them.

You probably have a specific set of skills and experience that can be very valuable for certain things. When you know your strengths, you can offer help that will add a lot of value. Saying no to something that you do not have the right skills or information also shows that if you were to help, then you are doing it for the right reasons. You are not trying to run away from your problems or trying to take control of other people's lives. This shows maturity and that you value your time. While you are willing to help others, you know that your time is worth something and would instead put it into something that will show results from what you have helped with.

Don't Help Individuals With Things They Can Do Themselves

You will get people who will just ask for help so that they do not have to lift a finger. If the task they ask for is something they could easily get done, you need to ask yourself why this person is asking for help. If you have been the type of person who just stayed and helped all the time, you might have these kinds of people in your life. They know that you have always been willing to help at a moment's notice, and that is what they are used to. It is your job to be assertive and tell them that you will no longer help with things they can do on their own.

This might sound harsh, but this is how people take advantage of you. Remember, you need to know that your time and energy is valuable. You will be more than happy to help with something that you can add value to. However, if someone is just trying to avoid their responsibilities, that is not a good enough reason for you to get involved. This is a very important thing to do when you first start making self-care a priority. Many people will still take chances with you because this is what they are used to, and you have to train them to treat you differently. You now see yourself differently, and it will take some time for other people to catch on.

Help Others Who Would Do the Same for You

When you are choosing people who you want to help, make sure that you choose wisely. Being there for being and assisting them should be a two-way street. I have seen so many people stick their neck out for people without it ever being reciprocated, which is a huge problem. While you should never help someone just to get something back, you cannot give all your time and resources to someone who will never do the same for you.

I often see this kind of scenario happen in the workplace. You will stay late to help one of your colleagues with something that has to be done, or you will stop what you are doing to help another person. Then, when it comes time for you to ask for help, in turn, that person is nowhere to be found. If someone always expects you to help them without ever helping you, they are just using you. You do not have a proper relationship with them, and they just see you as someone they can call on when they need assistance. If you notice this kind of pattern in your life, you need to decline helping these people.

Relationships are about give and take. If just one person is giving the whole time, the relationship will not work because it means that the taker is not someone who actually cares about you or values you. You need to know your worth enough to say no to these people. It's important to use your time, resources, and skills to help people who really appreciate it and who you have a real relationship with.

Setting Boundaries

When you offer your help to someone, one of the most important things is having the proper boundaries. When you have boundaries, you can feel safe that you are taken care of, and you are free to operate within the bounds you have set. Having clear boundaries also shows people what they can expect from you. This is beneficial to both you and others because everyone knows what to expect, and there will be no overcomplications.

Boundaries can come in many forms and can be implemented in many categories in your life. You are completely in control of your boundaries and how rigid they are. It is important to have your boundaries set before entering a situation where you have to use them. This will help you communicate clearly to others, and it will help you feel safer when you enter a situation where boundaries are necessary.

There are five different types of boundaries that you can set:

- **Financial** - This indicates what you will allow and won't allow where your finances are concerned. If you are saving for something, then your financial boundaries should be stricter. You will choose not to lend out money and will have a specific amount allocated to certain things. If people want to do something that will cost money, you will have to look at the financial boundaries before agreeing.
- **Emotional** - This has to do with your feelings. You might put up boundaries where you only open up and share with certain people. If there is someone who is prying and trying to dig too deep, you can put up your emotional boundaries by saying that

you do not feel comfortable with the conversation, then walk away.

- **Physical -** This includes your physical space, your body, and your privacy. If someone calls you up and asks if they can come crash in your house for a few weeks, and you have strong physical boundaries, you would say no because they would be invading your physical space, and that is something that you are not comfortable with.
- **Sexual -** It is important to have sexual boundaries so that you can communicate your expectations when it comes to intimacy with another person.
- **Intellectual** - This has to do with your thoughts or beliefs. If you are a religious person and someone asks you to do something that goes against what you believe, these boundaries can be put up to make sure that you only take part in the things you feel comfortable with.

The most important thing when it comes to setting boundaries is to make sure that you can communicate them effectively. As soon as something happens that makes you feel uncomfortable, or that is stepping over the boundaries you have set for yourself, you need to make it known. You do not need to go around and tell people your boundaries; just communicate with them in relevant situations. For example, if someone asks you to loan them money, but you have already decided that you are not comfortable with lending money to anyone, you can make these boundaries known to them. You do not have to explain why you have them. It just has to be clear to them that they do exist. Eventually, people will start to pick up on what you will and won't allow, and they will stop asking for things they know are outside of your boundaries.

Chapter 8:

Taking Responsibility For Others'

Happiness Hurts Them

The fundamental truth of life is that we are all responsible for our own happiness and that nobody else can help us find it or give it to us. This also means that you cannot be the one to give someone else their happiness. They have to do this on their own. No matter how much you give them and how much time you pour into them, there is nothing you can do if they are not willing to do something for themselves.

It can be so hard to see them not progressing or even wasting their lives away when you care about someone. This is when we usually like to take this responsibility and try to make things work for them. If you are working harder to make someone happy than what they are, you have to accept that this is not what they want. If people want something bad enough, they will get up and chase after it. If you try and get them to pursue happiness, it will be like pushing a giant boulder uphill. You will be expending all this energy and time, but you still won't really get anywhere. This is why it is so important to understand that happiness is only given to those who chase it down for themselves.

Everyone is on their own journey, and they have to be allowed to walk it. Right now, you are on a journey to find your own happiness and learn how to take care of yourself. It may not be an easy one, but it will be worth it. Nobody in the world can help you along the way; it's all up to you, and you have to be the one to put in the effort and make the changes for yourself. If you take things by the horns and do what you have to do, you will see the benefits of that. If someone else were to jump in and try and push you or take responsibility for what you need to do, you would never learn anything. You would probably stay stuck where you are and be unable to access the fantastic benefits of putting yourself first. In the same way, you shouldn't rob someone else of the experience they might get from doing it on their own and taking the responsibility they need to.

You Are Not Responsible For Others' Feelings

In the same way that you are not responsible for someone else's happiness, you are also not responsible for their feelings. In fact, sometimes it is actually better to hurt their feelings than try and preserve them. When we try so hard to spare people feelings, it can be a bad thing because it means that we could be dancing around the truth and not telling them what they need to hear. You need to be able to do your part, and how they take, it is up to them.

This does sound harsh, but you would never get anywhere if you cannot be direct with someone. Learning to be direct is a great skill to have, as it will cut down on the amount of misunderstanding you will have. This is especially important when you are communicating your boundaries or saying no to someone. When you do these things, you should not be thinking about how the other person is going to take it because that is not your responsibility. Instead, you have to focus on being clear with what you have to say. Once you have communicated what you need to, it is up to the other person to decide how they are going to handle it.

This does not give you free reign to be rude and careless. You should still try and be as kind as possible, but do not beat around the bush. Your communication should always be clear. Some people will take clarity at you being rude, and if this is the case, then that's just how it is. You do not have to feel guilty about it. If you are constantly focusing on other people, you will lower your boundaries and not say no. If someone gets extremely angry at you for communicating how you feel, this could be a sign of emotional manipulation, and you should not respond to this. Sometimes, it is just better to let things go, and this is one of those times.

This is why it is important to set your boundaries very early on. This will allow you to know what you will allow from people and what is not acceptable. For example, if someone acts in a way that you are not comfortable with, you can decide to walk away. This is also important for when someone asks something of you that you do not want to fulfill. Having boundaries in place from the beginning will help you navigate complex situations. For example, it will allow you to draw the line between being a helpful person and taking responsibility for another person's happiness while sacrificing your own.

Chapter 9:

How to Take Care of Yourself

We are all tasked with the responsibility to take care of ourselves. While this might sound like an easy task, a lot of work goes into it. We often take ourselves for granted because we are always with ourselves. We might think that we know what we need, but only when we spend intentional time getting to know ourselves will we know what we need. In this chapter, we will go over how we can take care of ourselves in the most effective way and make sure that we target all the important areas.

The 8 Different Areas of Taking Care of Yourself

Eight areas need to be focused on when you are thinking about self-care. Humans are multifaceted, which means multiple areas need to be paid attention to. You can't just take a spa day and think that you are fully taken care of. While a spa day is great, many other areas that will not benefit from a massage need to be attended to.

The other thing that is important to note is that self-care is all about balance, meaning that you have to give attention to all areas to feel fully happy and at peace. If one of these areas is off-balance, you should do your best to bring it back up again. You will feel your best when all eight areas are where they need to be.

Financial Self-Care

The first area that we will talk about is financial self-care, which is one of the areas that people most often skip. It doesn't seem like something you would do to take care of yourself because most people do not get joy from paying bills and creating budgets. However, while it may not be the most exciting part of self-care, it is one of the essential parts. When your finances are in order, you feel secure. Finances are a big part of all of our lives, and those who have all of their finances in order and are not stressed out about money are a whole lot happier.

You should aim to have a good relationship with money. If you have bills, make sure that they are being paid on time. If you are looking to make a big purchase, have a plan to save for it. If you are currently in debt, start taking steps toward paying it off as quickly as you can. All of these contribute to your financial health. If I were to give you one piece of advice that I want you to take for your finances, it would be to make sure that you do not spend more money than what you make. Budget according to what is coming into your bank account every month, and do your best to not go into debt.

When you are able to spend and save your money wisely, there will be so much less stress in your life. You will also be able to set your boundaries more clearly, and you will know how much money you have and how much you have to spend. There will be no guesswork when you are at the till and no sweating when you receive an unexpected bill because you have the savings to cover it. Financial stress is one of the worst out there, so what you can remove can make your life a whole lot happier and less complicated.

Physical Self-Care

This has to do with everything that impacts you physically and your physical health. When people think of self-care, the things that fall into this category will be the things that most often come to mind. For example, you could take a bath, visit your doctor, exercise, go for a massage, sleep, and eat the right foods to nourish your body. All of these things will be included in your physical self-care.

Physical self-care feeds into many other areas of self-care. If your body feels horrible, then it is tough to start working on other areas of your life. After all, you need to be physically able to do the different forms of self-care. So, if you are going to start improving your life at any point, I would suggest starting with physical self-care.

The activities that you do to take care of yourself physically also benefit other areas of self-care. Things like eating nutritious foods and exercising also have benefits for your emotional and psychological health. When your body feels good, you are more likely to feel good in other areas. Physical self-care is also relatively straightforward, and you will be able to see the benefits of it almost immediately. In contrast, other forms of self-care do take some time before you start to see benefits. If you are the type of person that is motivated by seeing results, then it would be the best option, to begin with, physical self-care.

Emotional Self-Care

When we speak about emotional self-care, we are referring to the way you feel. This is also how well you navigate through negative emotions, handle negative situations, manage stress, and how well you understand the reasons behind your feelings. It is crucial to be able to read your feelings because they will often lead you to more profound things that need your attention. For example, if you are upset about something, you can do a little digging and see what exactly about that situation made you upset. This might lead you to something that you could change or avoid in the future.

If you are taking care of your emotions properly, you will also be able to control them. Emotions are good things, but they can sometimes be a bit unpredictable, and you cannot base all of your decisions on them. Being able to control your emotions does not mean that you do not allow yourself to feel, but that you are able to not act out of them. For example, if something is making your blood boil, you would be able to calm your emotions down so that you can handle the situation as calmly as possible instead of blowing up and yelling. Once the situation has been handled, you can then go back and express what made you angry in a more mature manner. Emotional maturity is key when you are dealing with others.

I have already mentioned that taking care of your physical health is key to being healthy emotionally. Other things you could do are to make time to reflect on your feelings at the end of the day, know your emotional boundaries, journal, and practice self-compassion. All of these things help you to understand your emotions and express them in healthier ways.

Spiritual Self-Care

We all have beliefs and values that are ingrained into us. This could be due to our own experiences, searching for purpose and meaning, something that our parents have passed down to us, or things we have learned from the world around us. Our beliefs and values are core to who we are, and these things need to be honored. However, not everyone in the world has the same beliefs, so you cannot expect everyone to understand where you are coming from. The same goes for others. Nevertheless, it is important to respect what others believe because it is such a big part of who they are.

The activities that you do that will count as spiritual self-care will depend on what you believe. You might have to do a little soul searching and find what connects you most to your spiritual side. Things like prayer, meditations, reading religious texts, taking a walk-in nature, and going to places of worship are all great ways to take care of yourself spiritually. Another really important thing is to surround yourself with people who have the same beliefs as you. Having a like-minded community can increase your spirituality by miles, and it makes you feel more connected to your spiritual side. This does not mean that you cannot have friends and relationships outside of your spiritual nor religious group, but you should make sure that a few people in your circle share the same beliefs as you.

Psychological Self-Care

The physiological side of self-care is all about mindfulness and creativity. Physiological self-care is meant to help you get to know yourself a lot better, which is why expressing yourself and being creative is a big part of it. Your psychology is a big part of who you are, as it shows you who you think and why you like to do things the way you do. For example, people who are more creative love to be around things that inspire them, and they want to express their creativity in their relationships and in the things they do. On the other hand, more logical people will be deep thinkers who may not be all that loaded, but a lot is going on in their heads. They express themselves through things that make their brain work, like developing plans and challenging themselves to solve problems. If you understand your psychology, you will understand why you do the things that you do.

Physiological self-care will be the thing that helps you to understand yourself more—writing in a journal, reading books, and trying new things all fall into this category. Another thing that you can do is to try out a personality test, like the Myers-Briggs test or the Enneagram. These group people based on how they think and interact with things around them, and many people have found them helpful in understanding themselves. You can do the free versions online, but the paid versions are a lot more detailed and will give you a better idea of your psychology if you are interested in something like this.

Social Self-Care

Humans are social creatures. Even the most introverted person will need to have some social aspect in their lives in order to be balanced and happy. Completely isolating yourself is an expeditious way to make yourself sad and not be able to live out your full potential. On the other hand, being around people is fun, and we all need a little support every now and then. The key to social self-care is to have the right people around you and to make sure that your circle is easy to connect with.

Unlike other forms of self-care, social self-care is give-and-take. To have people be there for you, you would have to do the same for them. You cannot only be thinking of yourself when it comes to your relationships. If you want to maintain your relationships, you will have to make time to spend with others, honor the commitments you make with others, and make some sacrifices within reason. Relationships have the power to make your life great or miserable, which is why it is important to choose the right people to be close to. There is no such thing as a perfect relationship, but there are those that will be worth the ups and downs. A life that is filled with good relationships will be so much better than one that does not have them.

Professional Self-Care

Your professional self-care has to do with work and your career. Most of us spend most of the day at work, performing tasks so that we can provide for ourselves. If you are lucky then, your profession is something you feel called to and fulfills you. Not everyone has a job that ticks all these boxes, but you do not need a perfect job in order to be able to take care of yourself professionally. Some people have jobs because they allow them to do other things, they love by giving them the money they need. This is perfectly okay; you do not have to be in love with every aspect of your job. Even the most perfect job will be frustrating and stressful at some point. This is just how life is.

In order to be cared for at work, you need to have boundaries in place. Even if you have the world's best job, there is no way that you can just keep working for hours on end. You need to have a time where you stop and get some rest. Aside from the time that you block out for this, you will also need to take breaks in your day. One of these will be your lunch break, where you should eat a healthy and balanced meal. Working takes a lot of mental and physical energy, so make sure you are fooling yourself right.

You should also do your best to better yourself in your professional capacity. Attending professional development opportunities and taking the time to learn valuable skills will be very valuable to your career. The goal should be to keep learning and growing. You should aim to work your way up and keep improving.

Environmental Self-Care

Your environment is the space that you find yourself in. This might be your desk at work, your home, or anywhere else in which you spend a lot of time. Our environments have a big part to play in how we feel. Have you ever tried to work in a place that was so cluttered that you just didn't know where anything was? If you have, you would know how hard it is to concentrate in a space like this.

Each space you have will be designated for something different, meaning they should give off a different vibe. Your office space should be neat and organized so that you feel like you can be productive when you sit down. Your car should be clean so that you do not feel claustrophobic and disorganized when you are traveling. Your house should be a place where you can come home and do what you like. The different rooms in your home can also be tailored to your needs. For example, your bedroom could be relaxing and cozy, while your study/art room could be filled with creative pieces that inspire you. At the end of the day, you will have to decide how you feel when you are in that space. This will determine how well you will be able to accomplish what you need to in that environment.

Specific things that you can do to help with your environmental health are to keep your space organized and clean, take out your clothes and make sure that they are neat and ready for you, clean up after you have eaten a meal, and monitor how much time you spend on social media. The last one might leave you a bit confused, but social media and technology form part of our environment. If you are scrolling through social media, it is a place where you spend a lot of time, impacting how you feel. If you follow any pages that do not make you feel good about yourself, you should unfollow them. Your environment should be a safe space where you feel comfortable.

Create a Self-Care Plan

Your self-care plan is going to be completely unique to you. Every person is different, and everyone will need to focus on different areas of their lives to make their plan be the most effective for them. It is important to have a plan in place because it serves as a sort of commitment. We are more likely to follow through when things have been written down, and it also helps us know exactly what we have to do. We do not want to think about self-care on busy days, so it will be one less thing to think about if it is already planned out.

In order to create an effective self-care plan, you will have to consider all eight areas of self-care. I would suggest that you get out your notebook or open a document on your computer. You should carve out a bit of time to do this, as you might have to do some deep thinking. Do not rush through this because it is crucial that you do it properly. Once you have a solid self-care plan, you will not have to do it again. You will only have to do short check-ups to ensure that you are on track and that all areas of your life are staying as balanced as possible. If something is going a little bit wonky, you can take some time to focus on that area.

Once you have some time carved out for this, you can get started. Write down each of the eight areas and start evaluating yourself. You can go back to the last section and see if there are any red flags. Once you have evaluated yourself, you will be able to start making a plan for yourself. Write down one thing that you want to focus on in each area. Doing more than one can become overwhelming, and you will not want to keep up with the plan.

On the other hand, the chances are that there will be things going right in each area, so one point of improvement should be enough. Once you have mastered the thing in that area, you can try something else. The goal is to be as balanced as possible.

You should also take some time and highlight the weakness lost in each area. You might not have an area of concern for each area, but there will be one where you might need to improve on. Make a note of these things to know what you have to work on in the future. Besides all of this, you should be doing something you enjoy in each area. The main goal of self-care is to live a life that you are happy with and enjoy your life to the fullest, so take some time to pick out an activity or practice that you enjoy doing. Then, you can add this to your self-care plan.

Once you know what you want to do for your self-care plan, you need to structure it out. The best thing to do is add it to your daily schedule so that you have carved out some time for it each day or week, depending on the type of self-care and the activity. If you have it in your schedule, it becomes a commitment, and you are more likely to do it. You can have it in your calendar or set reminders on your phone or anything else that will remind you that it is time for self-care.

Remember to set aside a specific block of time for this and be realistic for the block of time you need.

When it comes to self-care, every day will not look the same, as you will not be able to do certain things all the time. For example, if you chose to go for a massage as your physical self-care activity, you will not be able to do this all the time. Going once a month will probably be enough for an activity like this. You will also have to factor in the times you will be going away on vacation and choosing to do other, bigger self-care activities. It will take some time to develop a plan that will work for you, and you will have to work through some trial and error before you find something suitable for your needs. Once you do, the process will become much easier, and you will feel so much better. You will likely see improvements in all eight areas, which will make you feel happy and balanced, which is the goal.

Chapter 10:

Remember, the First Person You

Need to Help is Yourself

I have mentioned multiple times throughout this book how helping yourself first is the priority. If you do not help yourself first, then you will not be able to help anyone else. You need to have control over your own life before you can even dream of looking into someone else's. In order to do this, you need to be able to recognize when people are just not worth helping. It can be tough to see the difference if you are a natural helper, but it is essential that you do.

Honestly, some people are not worth helping. These people will be a drain on your mental and physical resources. You should never feel wholly drained after helping someone, and if this is the case, you can take it as a red flag. If you are going to be able to take care of yourself in a sustainable way truly, you will need to stop helping those who are a drain on you.

When you are thinking about helping someone, you need to evaluate them and see if it will be worth it. You should not help someone who doesn't deserve your help. This is going to be difficult if you're the helping type, but stay strong. Not every person who asks for your support should get it. You are not a savior, so you cannot be physically and mentally exhausting yourself to extreme extents. However, your effort and expertise have value, and you need to know that. If you know that someone will not appreciate your help, you should not help them. These are the types of people who take advantage of them and just use them for their own gain. The thing is that showing appreciation is not a hard thing. A simple thank you and a small gift, depending on how much help they needed, is all it takes. If someone is not even willing to give you this, they are not the type of person you should go out of your way for.

Another indication that you should not be helping someone is if you cannot give your all to it, either physically or emotionally. If you do not have the time or resources to help out, there should be no need to help. You can politely decline so that they are free to find someone else. However, if you do not have the time or resources to help the person, you will just end up doing a lousy job, which is a waste for both of you. The other way you could not be able to give your all is emotionally. If you do not feel like helping at all, you need to honor your feelings. Your feelings usually point you to something bigger. Take the time to analyse why you are feeling a certain way. There might be a valid reason why you feel like this, and it is best just to decline to help. If you are not fully emotionally invested, you will not be able to do your best, so it is best to say that you cannot help.

When to Quit Helping People

You will have to make some tough calls in life. When it comes to your own health, you will have to put yourself first so that you do not suffer. This might mean that you have to say no to people or let them down. You should always keep your commitments unless you really feel like it is affecting you negatively. At the end of the day, you are your first priority, and if you feel that you are suffering somehow, then it is time to be honest with yourself and those that will be affected by your decision.

If It is Making You Unhappy

Naturally, we will want to do things for people who appreciate the effort we are putting in. This does play a significant factor in whether or not you wish to help someone, but this is not what will cause you to be unhappy when you are helping someone. Many things contribute to unhappiness when you are trying to give of yourself to help someone else. If you are feeling blue, you need to explore this more. Take some time to sit down and think about what is making you feel like this. You need to take some time to analyze feelings because the cause of the negative emotion is not always evident from the get-go.

When we offer to help someone, the relationship between you and that person sometimes might end up suffering. You should not work with some people, but we often do not know this until we get started. If you see that you are no longer as close to a person due to the help you are giving them, then you need to make the call to stop offering support. One of the most common areas this happens is with financial aid. When people loan others money, they will be waiting to be paid back for it. If the person who borrowed the money goes out for dinner or buys something that is not necessarily needed, the person who lent the money to them will likely be very suspicious of that. This can lead to bad blood between friends because the lender will constantly analyse how the borrower is spending their money. If you find that something similar is happening to you, you need to make a judgement call. Your relationships and your overall happiness are more important than the help that you are offering the person.

You should sit down with the person and do your best to explain the situation, making sure to let them know how you are feeling. If this is someone you are close to, it is even more vital to be transparent with them. It is unlikely that they have felt the tension in the relationship, and they will want to salvage it in any way they can. If you are offering help to someone you are not that close to, you do not have to be as open with your reasoning, but it is good to be as honest as you can about it.

You should always be selective about who you offer help to. You should not feel obligated to help everyone who asks you for help. You have the option to say no when it is necessary, which is even more important when it comes to financial assistance. Out of all the ways people could ask you for help, this one has a tremendous potential to go sour. If you feel a little bit uneasy with it, it is best to be cautious with it. My rule of thumb is never to lend money that you need for something else. There is always a chance that you could not get the money back, so if you are going to lend someone money, make sure it is a small amount and that it is something that you will not need back by a specified time.

You should also be clear about the parameters in which you can help. Sometimes you can offer some kind of help even if it is not the full help that the person is seeking. For example, if the person needs to borrow $500. If you are not comfortable lending them the whole amount but are willing to do something, you could offer to lend them $200. If you are happier with doing that, you can offer the person and see what they say. Remember that when someone is asking for help, it puts you in control of the situation. You have the power to say yes, no, or choose a way that will be better for you.

If You Feel Like You Are Being Exploited

If you have someone in your life who you have been helping for a long time, there is a chance that they are looking to just use you for what you can offer them. If you ever feel that you are being exploited somehow, you need to look into this. People often exploit kind and caring people because they know they can convince them to do what they need. If you feel used, then you have full right to remove yourself from the situation.

One of the things that you will have to keep an eye on is how people treat you when you are helping them. If you offer them something and they keep wanting more and seeking more help, then this can get too much for you and is a sign that the person is trying to get the most out of you as they can. You are not an item that must be squeezed out, for they are worth it. You have the power to step back and say no. Remember that as soon as you get a funny feeling about something or you feel like you are doing too much, then you can bailout.

When you are going to help someone, you must make sure that you are extremely clear about what you can offer. Lay it out on the table and leave it up to them. If they accept, you no longer have to be involved as soon as you are done with what you said you could do. They really can't say anything, and you can point them back to the original agreement if they do. Clear communication is vital when you are offering your help to someone.

Knowing how to help someone and what you can offer is all part of looking after yourself first. You are not saying that you cannot help them at all. You just know your boundaries and are willing to honor them.

Conclusion

I cannot stress enough how important it is to look after yourself first. It is actually one of the most important things you will ever do in your life. You will have many relationships, and people will come and go throughout your life, but you will always have you. The relationship you have with yourself is the most important relationship you will ever have, and if you do not take care of it, all other relationships will not work. Self-care is vital because it shows yourself the love and care you deserve so that you have something to give when you need to reach out to others. I hope that by now, you can see how unselfish self-care is.

Everything that you do impacts yourself in some way. It is crucial to be conscious of our thoughts and actions. If you are able to do this, you will be able to get to the root cause of your thoughts and actions and change them from there. It is essential to do this to get to know yourself better and make sure that any negative habits are changed to make them disappear permanently.

It is healthy to focus on yourself first, and you should never feel guilty for doing this. On the contrary, taking care of yourself should feel like joy and something that you love doing. I have learned how fulfilling life is when I take care of myself, and you will also see how much better your relationships are. They will be more prosperous and more valuable to you, and people will also start treating you with more value and respect. This is because you assign value to yourself, and other people follow your lead. If you know your worth, then so will other people.

Now that you have come to the end of the book, it is time to start taking action. Pick one or two things from the book that you can start working on. Go back to the chapters that really stuck out to you and pick something from there. It is going to be a journey, so don't expect your whole life to change overnight. You will have to put in the work, but once you do, you will start seeing the benefits of all the effort you put in. Eventually, you will look back and see how much you have grown and changed and be so proud of how far you have come. I know that you will be able to live the life that you deserve and see yourself as valuable as I know you are. I wish you all the luck on your journey as you learn how to start putting yourself first.

References

Andras, S. (2013, December 10). *7 ways to find out what you really want in life.* Lifehack. https://www.lifehack.org/articles/communication/7-ways-find-out-what-you-really-want-life.html

Baratta, M. (2018, May 27). *Self care 101.* Psychology Today. https://www.psychologytoday.com/us/blog/skinny-revisited/201805/self-care-101

Brzosko, M. (2018, February 28). *How to practice physical, mental, and emotional self-care.* Shine. https://advice.theshineapp.com/articles/how-to-practice-physical-mental-and-emotional-self-care/

Davis, T. (2018, December 28). *Self-Care: 12 ways to take better care of yourself.* Psychology Today. https://www.psychologytoday.com/za/blog/click-here-happiness/201812/self-care-12-ways-take-better-care-yourself

Diaz-Ortiz, C. (2013, May 1). *99 ways to say no*. Linkedin. https://www.linkedin.com/pulse/20130501190655-52397036-100-ways-to-say-no/

Dowling, D. (2016, March 13). *You are not responsible for other people's happiness*. Dr. Danielle Dowling. https://danielle-dowling.com/not-responsible-peoples-happiness

Johnson, J. (2020, December 18). *7 ways to focus on yourself*. Healthline. https://www.healthline.com/health/focus-on-yourself

Kohr, A. (2015, May 12). *10 simple ways to practice self-care (it's easier than you think)*. Wanderlust. https://wanderlust.com/journal/simple-ways-practice-self-care/

Leigh, S. (2019, October 7). *Fixing other people's problems*. Medium. https://shanleighwats.medium.com/fixing-other-peoples-problems-47aea2b46018

Martins, A. (2017, June 7). *Addicted to helping: Why we need to stop trying to fix people*. Tiny Buddha.

https://tinybuddha.com/blog/addicted-helping-why-we-need-stop-trying-fix-people/

Modern Therapy. (2018, October 25). *8 areas of self-care.* Modern Therapy. https://moderntherapy.online/blog-2/areas-of-self-care

Nandyz Soulshine. (2017, June 22). *5 reasons why learning to say no is an important life skill.* Nandyz Soulshine. https://nandyzsoulshine.com/saying-no-important-life-skill/

Nguyen, H. (2019, April 17). *To all the girls out there, everyone is responsible for their own happiness.* The Odyssey Online. https://www.theodysseyonline.com/responsible-for-their-your-happiness

Pattemore, C. (2021, June 3). *10 ways to build and preserve better boundaries.* Psych Central. https://psychcentral.com/lib/10-way-to-build-and-preserve-better-boundaries#10-tips

Perimeter Healthcare. (n.d.). *The importance of self-care.* Perimeter Healthcare. https://www.perimeterhealthcare.com/about/news/the-importance-of-self-care/

Pomerance, M. (n.d.). *This is why we constantly try to solve other people's problems.* The Candidly. https://www.thecandidly.com/2019/why-we-try-to-solve-other-peoples-problems-and-how-to-stop

Pratt, E. (2021, June 21). *Why (and how!) you need to pen in self-care.* Psych Central. https://psychcentral.com/blog/what-self-care-is-and-what-it-isnt#1

Quora. (n.d.). *Why is it easier to see and solve other people's problems than your own? Why is it so hard to use your own advice?* Quora. https://www.quora.com/Why-is-it-easier-to-see-and-solve-other-peoples-problems-than-your-own-Why-is-it-so-hard-to-use-your-own-advice

Restorative Counseling Chicago. (2018, August 21). *Is self-care selfish?* Restorative Counseling. https://rcchicago.org/self-care/

Ritchie, J. (2016, July 21). *Why we put ourselves last & why self-care should be a priority.* Tiny Buddha. https://tinybuddha.com/blog/why-put-ourselves-last-why-self-care-priority/

Sapala, L. (2020, May 8). *You're not responsible for other people's feelings.* IntrovertDear. https://introvertdear.com/news/youre-not-responsible-for-other-peoples-feelings/

Skills You Need. (2011). *Improving self-esteem.* Skills You Need. https://www.skillsyouneed.com/ps/self-esteem.html

Ward, D. (2014, January 11). *Why we help others instead of ourselves.* Psychology Today. https://www.psychologytoday.com/za/blog/sense-and-sensitivity/201401/why-we-help-others-instead-ourselves

World Health Organization. (2018, June 15). *What do we mean by self-care?* World Health Organization. https://www.who.int/news-room/feature-stories/detail/what-do-we-mean-by-self-care

Printed in Great Britain
by Amazon